International Journal for Religious Freedom (IJRF)
Journal of the International Institute for Religious Freedom

The IJRF aims to provide a platform for scholarly discourse on religious freedom and persecution. It is an inter-disciplinary, international, peer reviewed journal, serving the dissemination of new research on religious freedom and contains research articles, documentation, book reviews, academic news and other relevant items.

The editors welcome the submission of any contribution to the journal. Manuscripts submitted for publication are assessed by a panel of referees and the decision to publish is dependent on their reports. The IJRF is listed on the DoHET "Approved list of South African journals" and subscribes to the Code of Best Practice in Scholarly Journal Publishing, Editing and Peer Review of 2018 as well as the National Code of Best Practice in Editorial Discretion and Peer Review for South African Scholarly Journals and the supplementary Guidelines for Best Practice of the Forum of Editors of Academic Law Journals in South Africa.

The IJRF is freely available online: www.iirf.eu, as a paid print subscription, and via SABINET.

Subscriptions 2016

Annual subscription fee:
SA Rand 300
VAT and postage included.
See subscription form in the back.

For international payments use:
http://iirfct.givengain.org
(pay in Rand!)

Bank details
Beneficiary: International Institute for Religious Freedom, Cape Town · Bank: Standard Bank · Branch: Sea Point
Branch Code: 02 41 09 · Account Number: 071 117 431
SWIFT Code: SBZAZAJJ

IJRF · P.O. Box 1336 · Sun Valley 7985 · Rep South Africa
Tel +27-21 783 0823 · Fax +27-86 551 6432 · editor@iirf.eu

International Institute for Religious Freedom (IIRF)
of the World Evangelical Alliance

www.iirf.eu

Friedrichstr. 38
2nd Floor
53111 Bonn
Germany
Bonn@iirf.eu

PO
Sur
Cap
Sou
Cap

D1673885

International Journal for Religious Freedom

Volume 8, Issue 1, 2015

ISSN 2070-5484
ISBN 978-3-86269-208-8

Acknowledgement of Sponsors
We would like to thank the sponsors who supported the editing, printing and distribution of this issue of IJRF. Their views and opinions are not necessarily those of IIRF and vice versa.

· Evangelical Lutheran Church in Württemberg, Germany www.elk-wue.de/landeskirche/international-information-en/
· Gebende Häude (Giving Hands), www.gebende-haende.de

Subscribe to get IJRF via email (time delayed – 1 March; 1 September)

➢ To receive new issues of IJRF electronically on release, send an email to: subscribe-ijrf-fulltext-subscribe@bucer.eu

➢ To receive an email notice about a new issue of IJRF available online, send an email to: subscribe-ijrf-notice-subscribe@bucer.eu

Note to librarians: IJRF is also available as an ePublication from Sabinet (www.sabinet.co.za). The first full volume of IJRF appeared in 2009. There was only one pilot issue in 2008.

Typesetting: Ben Nimmo (Solid Ground), www.solidground.training

Cover art: Julene Fast. Photo credit: St Jacobs Printery
Every year, Mennonites hold a quilt auction to raise funds for the work of the Mennonite Central Committee, the relief, service, development and peace agency of Mennonites in Canada. This feature quilt was made by Julene Fast of the Hawkesville Mennonite Church. It was sold at the New Hamburg Mennonite Relief Sale. Mennonites are an Anabaptist Christian minority group that has been persecuted in many countries. They are known for their pacifist beliefs and for their work in relief and development. An article in this journal explicates some of their history in Canada, where they have sought refuge.

Contents

International Journal for Religious Freedom
Volume 8, Issue 1/2, 2015

ISSN 2070-5484

Christians under Pressure: Studies in Discrimination and Persecution 1

Bernhard Reitsma (Ed.)

Fruitful Minorities

The Witness and Service of
Christian Communities in
Predominantly Islamic Societies

VKW

Editorial

We're Back on Track

There is great rejoicing as the *International Journal for Religious Freedom* is finally being published again! As the *IJRF* is an open-access journal, many have noticed that it has been effectively dormant since 2014. It has been a big effort to get this issue out and we are happy to introduce the new managing editor, Prof Dr Janet Epp Buckingham, who is bringing the journal back to life!

She is a Canadian university professor with a long history of work promoting religious freedom. She has been an advocate with the World Evangelical Alliance in Geneva and an advocate to Global Affairs Canada. As well, she has been associated with the International Institute for Religious Freedom since its inception and served on the advisory board of this journal.

We equally express our warmest thanks to our new language editor Bruce Barron, PhD, and longstanding proofreader Barbara Felgendreher, MA, and typesetter Ben Nimmo.

Yours for religious freedom, Prof Dr Christof Sauer
and Prof Dr Dr Thomas Schirrmacher, editors

Christian minorities and religious freedom

This issue represents the geographical and interdisciplinary breadth that the journal strives for, with articles ranging from law to theology and from Nigeria to North America. While there was no preconceived thematic focus, the uniting thread of most of the contributions is a focus on Christian minorities and religious freedom. Thomas Schirrmacher's opinion essay on laws relating to loudspeakers on minarets is part of an ongoing dialogue on this issue.

Leah Farish draws on surveys of Moroccan Christians to describe in detail their experiences of living in a Muslim country. My article on the history of separatist Anabaptist Christians in Canada explores a similar experience of life as a religious minority, but through the lens of legal cases. I contrast political promises of accommodation of religious practices with the less favourable reality and ensuing legal challenges.Emmanuel Osewe Akubor discusses in depth the rise of fundamentalist Islamic groups in northern Nigeria and their impact on Christian minorities in that region.

Nicholas Kerton-Johnson and Tom Simmons have contributed articles on religious freedom issues in the US. Kerton-Johnson focuses on the theology of persecution and how Christians and churches should and should not respond to being marginalized. Although he discusses the US situation specifically, his theological approach is applicable to a variety of contexts. Simmons reviews the *Hobby Lobby* decision of the US Supreme Court and considers the implications of granting religious freedom to corporate entities.

Three of the articles in this issue feature the ongoing tensions, sometimes leading to persecution, between Muslims and Christians. Accordingly, Carsten Polanz's review essay on the Muslim concept of *takfir* is an important contribution to our understanding. The essay is based on two books exploring this topic.

Thomas Schirrmacher has contributed an extended review and commentary on Michael Schwartz's book on ethnic cleansing. Other reviews cover books on Turkish martyrs and on the theology of persecution.

Some of the articles in this issue were submitted in 2015 so you will find that they are current as of the date of the issue. Some articles have references after 2015, because they were submitted for publication after the 2015 date. We did not ask authors to revise. This issue went to press in early 2020. We trust you will still find this issue interesting and valuable.

Prof Dr Janet Epp Buckingham, managing editor

Publishers: Want to advertise a book? Want your book listed under "Books Received"?
Reviewers: Want to review a book?
bookreviews@iirf.eu

The use of loudspeakers for the Islamic call to prayer
An infringement upon negative religious freedom?
Thomas Schirrmacher[1]

Keywords   Switzerland, muezzin, church bells.

1. An important distinction

The question of whether Muslims are allowed to build a minaret and the question of whether a muezzin is allowed to use a loudspeaker five times a day for a call to prayer must to be clearly distinguished from each other.[2] Within the framework of religious freedom, the construction of minarets is allowed in Germany. The range of protection provided by Article 4 of Germany's Basic Law does not differentiate based on the numerical strength or social relevance of a religious association.[3] The construction of minarets therefore follows the foundational idea of equal treatment. The same principle applies to the issue of what building limitations can be placed upon churches and other religious structures (e.g. location, use, height, number of parking spaces). In these decisions, fair consideration must be given equally to new construction of large churches and to smaller churches.

Let us turn our attention exclusively to the call to prayer. The Swiss newspaper *Schweizer Tagesanzeiger* writes poignantly, "The minaret is an elevated portion of a mosque, from which a muezzin calls believers to pray five times a day and glorify Allah. In most cases, a minaret is a tower. Nowadays, a muezzin mostly does this

---

[1] Thomas Schirrmacher (* 1960) is an international human rights expert and chair of the International Council of the International Society for Human Rights, Associate Secretary General of the World Evangelical Alliance and director of the International Institute for Religious Freedom (Bonn, Cape Town, Colombo). He is professor of the sociology of religion at the State University of the West in Timisoara in Romania and Distinguished Professor of Global Ethics and International Development at William Carey University in Shillong (Meghalaya, India). Schirrmacher earned four doctorates in Theology (Dr. theol., 1985, Netherlands), in Cultural Anthropology (PhD, 1989, USA), in Ethics (ThD, 1996, USA), and in Sociology of Religions (Dr. phil., 2007, Germany) and received two honorary doctorates in Theology (DD, 1997, USA) and International Development (DD, 2006, India). Article received: 19 Sept. 2015; Accepted: 26 Sept. 2015. Contact: Friedrichstr. 38, 53111 Bonn, Germany, Fax +49 2289650389, Email: DrThSchirrmacher@me.com.

[2] As far as I can see, the so-called Swiss Minaret Initiative, a law voted in by the majority of the voters against the will of the government that banned the building of minarets, deliberately did not keep both of these questions apart but rather combined them.

[3] See Martin Völpel. *Streitpunkt Gebetsruf: Zu rechtlichen Aspekten im Zusammenhang mit dem lautsprecherunterstützen Ruf des Muezzin* (Bonn: Die Bundesregierung/ Federal Government, 1997), 26.

over a loudspeaker since his voice would otherwise not be heard over the noise of the traffic – and in so doing the minaret fulfils the same function as a church tower with a bell."[4]

In such case, all limitations placed on bell ringing would apply equally to the amplified call to prayer issued from a minaret. As Claus-Dieter Classen states, a regulation can "only be uniformly applied to all religions. ... The muezzin's call can thus not be allowed to experience an essentially more restrictive treatment than Christian bells."[5] But I am not sure that the two situations are truly equal. In my view, the muezzin, in making a verbal confession of faith, compels other people to participate in the exercise of another religion five times a day. As a result, this case touches upon the concept of negative religious freedom.

Admittedly, this issue is disputable, and I am not a legal specialist. Rather, I view the issue primarily from the point of view of a sociologist and a human rights activist. Nevertheless, I want to start a discussion on this important topic.

2. Do legal limitations on the use of church bells and on the calls of muezzins deny basic rights?

It is not possible to limit a guaranteed basic right to religious freedom on any basis other than by applying another basic right that is guaranteed in the constitution. This principle applies all over the world, although for simplicity I will stick with the German case in this essay.

Because of the fundamental right to religious freedom, no religious community is required to comply with permissible religious noise levels, as would be the case with non-religious facilities. A mosque thus needs no operating license for its muezzin to make calls to prayer through a loudspeaker. Legal clarification of a matter becomes possible when someone lodges a complaint after a practice has been started.

In Article 140 of Germany's Basic Law, which derives from Article 137, Paragraph 3, Sentence 3 of the Weimar Constitution (the 1919 German constitution), one finds these words: "Every religious community administers its own affairs within the frame of the general laws valid for all. It appoints its officials without the particpation of the State or the civil community." According to Sentence 1 of Article 137, a religious community must be officially recognized to qualify for this protection.

In Germany, the Federal Emission Control Act (Bundes-Immissionsschutzgesetz, or BImSchG) provides the legal framework for permitting and controlling noise generation. (The longer name for this law is translated as "Federal Act on the Pre-

---

4   "Allahs Türme" (2009), available at https://www.nzz.ch/allahs_tuerme-1.3884276 (2009).
5   Claus-Dieter Classen, *Religionsrecht* (Tübingen: Mohr Siebeck, 2006), 162–163 (paragraph 390).

vention of Harmful Effects on the Environment caused by Air Pollution, Noise, Vibration and Similar Phenomena." It is Germany's most important environmental law.) It can be applied to church bells only when they are fulfilling a so-called worldly function (for instance, pealing to indicate the time of day).[6] In the case of a muezzin, there is no worldly noise; all the muezzin's calls are religious in nature. Moreover, one can take action against the pealing of bells or the muezzin's calls through a loudspeaker only to protect other rights, such as the right to inviolability, which takes effect if the noise generation is so loud that it negatively impacts one's health.[7] To state it in another way, our justice system distinguishes between *liturgical* bell ringing (for instance, at the beginning of a worship service or during the time when the community of believers is repeating the Lord's Prayer) and *worldly* or secular ringing (e.g. a fire alarm or a public clock or when marking political events). Worldly bell ringing might enjoy a certain protection as an old tradition. However, it is generally subject to normal laws, for which reason a citizen can bring a civil suit to stop it, whereas one cannot do so to prevent liturgical bell ringing. This activity is essentially protected unless it infringes upon other basic rights, and even then some sort of balance has to be sought between the conflicting rights.[8] The practical ramifications can be illustrated by an example related to volume. The worldly ringing of bells, like all forms of public noise generation, is subject to the allowable reference values contained in the Technical Guidelines for Noise Prevention (Technische Anleitung zum Schutz gegen Lärm, or TA Lärm). In contrast, these reference values do not apply to the liturgical ringing of bells, which can be louder, although there is naturally a limit here if the bells cause adverse health effects for others.

Such a differentiation does not apply in the case of the calls made by a muezzin. In his case, there are only calls made in a liturgical form. "The call of the muezzin has solely a ritual significance and corresponds to the liturgical ringing of bells. For that reason, it cannot generally be prohibited, but according to each situation there are constraints which can be imposed."[9] That the call of the muezzin is not yet under administrative jurisdiction has to do only with the fact that Muslim groups are not yet bodies under public law – and there are already exceptions to this, such as the Ahmadiyyas in the state of Hesse.

Ansgar Hense has listed which rights at the constitutional level could limit the right to religious freedom in the case of bell ringing:

---

[6] See Gerhard Czermak, *Religions- und Weltanschauungsrecht* (Berlin and Heidelberg: Springer-Verlag, 2008), 233 (paragraph 441).

[7] Classen, *Religionsrecht*, 162 (paragraph 388).

[8] Czermak, *Religions- und Weltanschauungsrecht*, 233–234 (paragraphs 441–442).

[9] Czermak, *Religions- und Weltanschauungsrecht*, 234 (paragraph 443).

1. The protection of life and physical integrity (Article 2, Paragraph 2, Sentence 1 of the Basic Law), in the case of too much noise generation;
2. Only in a very limited way: the right to general freedom of action (Article 2, Paragraph 1 and Article 14 of the Basic Law);
3. In an even more limited way: the prohibition against impairment of property, such as when a neighboring piece of property loses value;
4. Finally, negative religious freedom.[10]

Since in every case only the last of these rights would apply, whereas the first three can be claimed only in a concrete, local case and must be reviewed individually, I will focus on negative religious freedom in the following discussion.

3. On negative religious freedom

On one hand, negative religious freedom arises implicitly from the right to freedom of religion and worldview (Article 4, Paragraph 1 of the Basic Law, the "Grundgesetz", the name of the Constitution of Germany).[11] The right to choose and exercise one's own religion or non-religious worldview naturally includes not being compelled to exercise any religion.

Additionally, a special type of negative religious freedom appears in Article 140 of the Basic Law (derived from Article 136, Paragraph 4 of the Weimar Constitution): "Nobody may be forced to participate in a religious act or festivity, to join in religious practices or to swear a religious oath."

Since no one is required to participate directly in the exercise of religion in the case of the call to prayer, just as in response to the ringing of bells, Martin Völpel denies the applicability of even this special form of negative freedom, contending that there is no "freedom from the religious exercise of others."[12] Granted, the muezzin's call entails no direct or even coerced participation. However, there is involuntary contact with the call to prayer through one's eyes and ears.

The Federal Constitutional Court has judged, with respect to public religious symbols, that merely seeing a religious item does not force anyone to participate in the exercise of religion: "In a society which provides space for various forms of faith convictions, there is no right for the citizen to be spared from professions of other faiths, ritualistic actions, and religious symbols."[13] The right to conduct mission activities also includes disseminating one's own faith publicly, such as on placards and displays or via street preachers.

---

[10] Ansgar Hense, Glockenläuten und Uhrenschlag. Der Gebrauch von Kirchenglocken in der kirchlichen und staatlichen Rechtsordnung (Berlin: Duncker and Humblot, 1998), 259.
[11] For a discussion, see Hense, *Glockenläuten und Uhrenschlag,* 278–282.
[12] Völpe, *Streitpunkt Gebetsruf,* 19; see also 20.
[13] BVerG93, 1/16 (judgement dated 24 September 2003); see Hense. *Glockenläuten und Uhrenschlag,* 279.

Repetitions	Wording of the Adhān	English Translation	Comment
4x	Allāhu akbar	Allah (God) is great (greater than anything and can be compared with nothing else).	Malikite legal school repeats only twice
2x	Ašhadu an lā ilāha illā llāh	I testify that there is no God except Allah (God).	–
2x	Ašhadu anna Muḥammad-an rasūlu llāh	I testify that Muhammad is the messenger of Allah (God).	–
2x	Ḥayya 'alā ṣ-ṣalāh	Hurry to prayer.	–
2x	Ḥayya 'alā l-falāḥ	Hurry to well-being (salvation, prosperity).	–
[2x]	Ḥayya 'alā ḫayri l-'amal	The time for the best deeds has come.	Exclusively used by Shiites
2x	aṣ-ṣalātu ḫayrun mina n-naum	Prayer is better than sleep.	Exclusively used by Sunnis (only at morning prayer)
2x	Allāhu akbar	Allah (God) is great (greater than anything and can be compared with nothing else).	–
1x	Lā illāha illā llāh	There is none worthy of worship except Allah (God).	Repeated twice by Shiites

I think, however, that the call by a muezzin is somewhat different. The crux of Islamic doctrine from the Koran, which declares that there is only one God and that Muhammad is his prophet, is expressed in the core statements "Allahu akbar" ("God is greater" or "God is greatest") and "la illaha illa-llah" ("there is no God except Allah"). Both are components of the daily prayer conducted five times per day (Arabic *salāt*) and of the Friday prayer in mosques and are also components of the muezzin's call (*adhān*). The content of the muezzin's call is described in the table above.

The muezzin's call thus contains the core of Islamic belief. Therefore, one must ask whether this is truly parallel to the ringing of bells, considering that the muezzin announces a direct confession of faith that everyone must hear five times per day. Moreover, does it make a difference that this confession additionally differentiates the Islamic faith from other religions – including specifically from Christianity? Does it make a difference that this confession rejects other religions and that everyone must hear it five times a day so that it is unwillingly internalized and then repeatedly comes to one's mind, like an 'earworm', even when the muezzin is not making the call to prayer?

A more suitable parallel to the muezzin's call would be if Christians were to sing the Apostles' Creed audibly and understandably through a loudspeaker from church towers until the church's neighbours could not get the song out of their head.

In my opinion, Gernot Facius correctly describes the difference: "Bells do not 'convey' any particular message. On the contrary, the muezzin calls out a confession of faith in public."[14] In the end, how the Islamic call to prayer is assessed will depend on whether this call, as a formulated confession of faith in which non-Muslims must also participate, infringes upon negative religious freedom, or whether this claim is denied either by saying that merely listening does not violate negative religious freedom or by arguing that non-Muslim Germans don't understand Arabic anyway.

4. Dispensing with the loudspeakers?

The call of the muezzin is a necessary component of the Islamic faith, but amplification through loudspeakers is not. From an Islamic point of view, one could do away with the amplification without making the prayer invalid.

For example, the call by a muezzin is often dispensed with in Indonesia, the world's largest Islamic country by population. Instead, the sound of gongs is used. In Marseille, France, the Muslim community has also discontinued the muezzin's call at its large mosque and instead sends a strong light signal to summon the people to prayer. In countries or areas where no public call to prayer is allowed, the call is made within the mosque at a moderate volume.

5. Excerpts from statement to the German Parliament

I will close by reproducing portions of a statement I made to the Bundestag (the German Parliament) on this topic:[15]

There is no human right which applies in an unlimited manner. The dignity of a human being is expressed in many respects, and they are to be collectively

---

[14] Gernot Facius, "Der Ruf des Muezzins und die Glocke," *Die Welt*, 17 April 2001, http://www.welt.de/print-welt/article445567/Der-Ruf-des-Muezzins-und-die-Glocke.html.

[15] For the full statement, see "Gemeinsamer Fragenkatalog für die öffentliche Anhörung des Ausschusses für Menschenrechte und humanitäre Hilfe des Deutschen Bundestages am 27.10.2010 zum Thema 'Religionsfreiheit und europäische Identität,'" https://www.thomasschirrmacher.info/wp-content/uploads/2012/09/Schirrmacher-Fragenkatalog-Menschenrechtsausschuss-27102010-dritte-Fassung.pdf.

acknowledged and implemented. There is no religious justification for child slavery or for getting around the prohibition against torture.

Insofar as international and European human rights standards are concerned, "encroachments" and "limitations", respectively, in fundamental human rights are only allowed on the basis of a general law. (For instance, that was the foundation for the ruling made by the Federal Constitutional Court on the question of whether Muslim teachers in Bavaria are allowed to wear a headscarf. There was no corresponding law in Bavaria. In the meantime, this has been rectified.)

In such questions of limiting religious freedom in the case of conflict with other rights, the European Court of Human Rights has often ruled altogether very favourably and in a differentiating manner.[16] In the process, it has involved limitations owing to public safety, public order, public health, and protection of the rights and freedoms of others.

With Islam, for reasons of equal treatment, a balance between religious freedom and other rights would have to occur. The only thing is that as far as the form of organization or support for a foundational democratic order is concerned, Islam does not bring along a historical accretion of preconditions over long stretches of time. At this point, equal treatment does not only have to occur formally. Rather, it also has to likewise encompass all content-related and other preconditions which, for example, churches have to fulfil.

Additionally, one cannot forget that in our country there are many laws touching upon moral questions and structures which have either been established against the will of the Christian religious community or go back to hard-won compromises. Why should it be any different for the Islamic religious community? Why should they experience no such incursion and for their part achieve in expedited proceedings what churches over the centuries and in recent decades have had to shed their skin for?

This also applies to building measures undertaken by various religions. It has to be a matter of equal treatment, whereby in the process Islamic mosque communities should not only compare themselves with mainstream Christian denominations, the large churches of which were almost all completely built in earlier times. Rather, they should compare themselves with Christian free churches, which also cannot build on every street corner, but must often search a long time for a suitable location on account of many constraints. Building laws and their implementation via democratically legitimate municipalities can also be applied to religious buildings, even if they are not able to prohibit religious buildings per se. In this respect, Muslims have to understand that in the case of approval to build mosques there can be delays, just as would be the case for every other religion or for every build-

---

[16] All judgements by this court are discussed in Daniel Ottenberg, *Der Schutz der Religionsfreiheit im Internationalen Recht* (Wiesbaden: Nomos, 2009), 138–182.

ing of such a size. Thus, a Swiss village could by all means protect the historical village image and recommend a permissible height for all buildings, including the building height of a minaret or its location, which would not obstruct the image taken in when viewing a historic village.

However, to essentially prohibit particular religious communities from having certain conspicuous building elements, and to do so at the level of the constitution, as is the case in Switzerland, infringes upon religious freedom. This was possible up to now only under Swiss direct democracy, where a voice of protest from the population can break new ground in a direct manner. It is significant to note that the Swiss minaret initiative[17] was backed neither by the government nor by any organized religious community. Also, the association of evangelical free churches, named the Swiss Evangelical Alliance, spoke out in opposition to the minaret initiative and against a prohibition on minarets. I have already critically pointed out that the Swiss minaret initiative, as far as I am able to survey its extent, has deliberately not distinguished between the construction of minarets and calls to prayer using loudspeakers. (By the way, the European Court of Human Rights will presumably annul the law one of these days.)

---

[17] A well-researched work on the minaret initiative in Switzerland is Vincenzo Pacillo, "'Stopp Minarett'? The Controversy over the Building of Minarets in Switzerland: Religious Freedom versus Collective Identity," in Silvio Ferrari and Sabrina Pastorelli (eds.), *Religion in Public Spaces: A European Perspective* (Ashgate, UK: Franham, 2012), 337–352.

Send your opinion piece to
editor@iirf.eu

Moroccan Christians
Lost Opportunities
Leah Farish[1]

Abstract

Thirty-two Moroccan Christians were surveyed about their lives in this Muslim king-dom, including their current lifestyle, church involvement, family life and aspirations for the future. Government restrictions on their freedom of speech and association as well as societal pressure to conform to Islam keep them from growing in numbers but also hold them back from volunteerism, educational and employment opportunities, planning for their own and their children's future, and participation in building civil society. The resulting limitations on their commercial activities and social networks impede Morocco's overall development.

Keywords   Religious freedom, economic development, persecution, Morocco.

1. Methodology

In this study, 32 Moroccan Christian adult citizens were interviewed using a protocol of open-ended questions about their life under Moroccan rule. Legal prohibitions, combined with Moroccan Christians' experience of social ostracism, workplace discrimination, and government suspicion and punishment, made these interviews difficult to conduct and somewhat risky for the participants. Therefore, surnames were not required of participants, and the surveyor is remaining anonymous to ensure future freedom of movement within Morocco.

The first nine and the last three interviews were conducted orally in person by the main surveyor, from a written script, with simultaneous translation by a church member who is also a professional translator. The others were conducted orally by the translator, and the translations were sent by email to the surveyor, who occasionally asked a clarifying follow-up question where needed. The respondents included primary and secondary school teachers, a university professor, an engineer, a physician, homemakers, labourers and small business owners. Except for the last

[1]   Leah Farish, BA, MA, JD, is an award-winning American civil rights attorney and adjunct professor at Oklahoma Wesleyan University. Email: leahfarish@gmail.com. She is an Honor Guard attorney with Alliance Defending Freedom and has published several scholarly articles on First Amendment issues. Ms. Farish has advocated for years concerning human rights issues in Morocco, speaking at the United Nations and college campuses around the United States. An earlier version of this article appeared as https://www.religiousfreedominstitute.org/cornerstone/2016/7/26/how-do-you-sur-vive-your-life-with-christ-moroccan-christians-speak. Three additional surveys completed since then are included in the present article. Article received: 17 August 2019; accepted: 11 January 2020.

group, these livelihoods are not strongly oriented to entrepreneurship, so they may perhaps not fully portray the extent of missed opportunities for economic development by and among Moroccan Christians nationwide. According to the US Department of State, other religious minorities experience many of the same problems as do Christians,[2] but those are beyond the scope of this article.

I will show how the opportunities desired by Moroccan Christians relate to the "pathways" identified by Anthony Gill and Timothy Shah.[3] According to Gill and Shah, these pathways, or models, are elements of religious freedom that benefit secular societies as well as the religious adherents themselves. Six of these elements will be explained and applied to the survey answers gleaned: religious activity as economic activity, growth-promoting religious ideas, charitable giving, migratory magnet, networks and voluntary associations, and civic skills.

2. Demographic and legal background

Recent estimates of the number of Christians in Morocco vary between 16,000 and 40,000.[4] One Moroccan pastor estimated that 80 percent of Moroccan Christians are Berber (or Amazigh, "free people"), who originally lived in the mountains of Morocco but are now scattered throughout the kingdom, and who were predominantly Jewish or Christian for centuries until Islam was imposed.

The religious practices of foreign residents – probably upwards of 30,000 foreigners are living in Morocco – are accommodated. They are given more latitude, although a large deportation and property seizure of foreign nationals accused of proselytizing was carried out in March 2010.[5]

Moroccan law forbids offering "enticements" to conversion,[6] or even "shaking the faith of a Muslim."[7] "Causing harm" to Islam can lead to imprisonment.[8] Vol-

---

[2] US Department of State, "2018 Report on International Religious Freedom: Morocco," https://www.state.gov/reports/2018-report-on-international-religious-freedom/morocco/.

[3] Anthony Gill and Timothy Shah, "Religious Freedom, Democratization, and Economic Development: A Survey of the Causal Pathways Linking Religious Freedom to Economic Freedom and Prosperity and Political Freedom and Democracy," presented at the Annual Meeting of the Association for the Study of Religion, Economics, and Culture, Washington, D.C., 13 April 2013, http://www.asrec.org/wp-content/uploads/2015/10/Gill-Shah-Religious-freedom-democratization-and-economic-development.pdf.

[4] The estimate of 16,000 comes from the page on Morocco at the Pew-Templeton's Global Religious Futures Project website, http://www.globalreligiousfutures.org/countries/morocco/religious_demography#/?affiliations_religion_id=0&affiliations_year=2010. The U.S. State Department has given the higher figure.

[5] Paul Marshall, Lela Gilbert and Nina Shea, "Persecuted: The Global Assault on Christians" (digital, Thomas Nelson, 2013).

[6] US Department of State, "2018 Report."

[7] Marshall, Gilbert and Shea, "Persecuted."

[8] Human Rights Watch, "Morocco/Western Sahara - Events of 2017," https://www.hrw.org/world-

untary change of religious affiliation is purportedly allowed, but in practice many converts to Christianity undergo government interrogation and surveillance, and ostracism by friends and co-workers, usually without recourse to assistance from law enforcement.[9] Although the constitution guarantees everyone the freedom to "practice his religious affairs," usually those affairs do not include – at least for Christians – proselytizing, obtaining a marriage license, avoiding Islamic indoctrination in public school, starting Christian schools, colleges or orphanages, conducting public baptisms, naming children with Christian names,[10] or obtaining visas to leave the country.

Black African believers seem to be given more freedom than Berber or Arab converts, possibly (and ironically) due to an anti-black prejudice[11] that tends to treat sub-Saharan Africans as somewhat irrelevant to the rest of society.

As a claimed descendant from the Prophet Muhammad, Morocco's popular King Mohammed VI is a staunch defender of the Muslim faith. Exceptions to freedom of speech guarantees include any criticism of the king or of state institutions.[12]

3. Survey responses

3.1 Religious activity as economic activity

Survey participants were asked, "In what ways would your church or ministry be different without state restrictions?" Nine said they would have a building for their church,[13] and six said they would like to have a place to hold large gatherings or "to welcome Muslim friends" such as a café or recreation center. Some didn't indicate a desire for a church building specifically, but just for a place to go and "pray any time."

Interestingly, six respondents said that their church would start a business to help support itself – an idea that Western churches rarely entertain. Several participants aspired to offer "job training" to others, and nine said that they would open a school.

Another question asked, "Would you feel more confident in developing business contacts, expanding your own business, investing in business projects, and/or being a leader in your workplace if you felt your religious views were protected?" Of

---

report/2018/country-chapters/morocco/western-sahara.

[9] US Department of State, "2018 Report," Section III.

[10] US Department of State, "2018 Report," Executive Summary.

[11] Susan Abulhawa, "Confronting Anti-Black Racism in the Arab World," *Al-Jazeera*, 7 July 2013, http://www.aljazeera.com/indepth/opinion/2013/06/201362472519107286.html; Mona Eltahawy, "The Arab World's Dirty Secret," *New York Times*, 10 November 2008, http://www.nytimes.com/2008/12/10/opinion/10iht-edeltahawy.1.18556273.html?_r=0.

[12] Human Rights Watch, "Morocco/Western Sahara," 8.

[13] Sadly, one said that a building would only become a target, and that Moroccan society was "not ready" for people to "be different."

the 32 respondents, 21 said yes, many of them enthusiastically. Negative responses included "I don't do business"; "No – I feel scared to do such business"; and "When people find I am a Christian, they won't do business with me." One of the affirmative respondents clarified that at this time, she does business only with Christians. One said he wanted to own a small sports center for children. Such centres are fairly common in the cities of Morocco; some are nonprofit and some are for-profit businesses. These instances reveal what Gill and Shah call "religious liberty not just as a good in its own right but as a wider economic … force."[14]

Christians don't feel confident that they or their workplaces are fully protected by law,[15] and this perception may be an obstacle to commercial activity. When asked if they would feel comfortable contacting law enforcement if they or fellow church members were victims of violent or discriminatory acts, 14 said no and two were not sure. One said she would obtain justice if she had been physically injured but would have no recourse if the injury were "just words." One said she would not contact law enforcement, because "Maybe it would cause more problems." Another person said she can't "talk to her co-workers" and that if she "sees injustice, it's hard to ignore."

Like everyone else, Christians love to express themselves. One woman said she would like to start a newsletter, stating confidently that she is "a good writer." Nine other respondents said they would start literacy classes, a school, a counseling center, parenting classes or other expressive activity. One said that a new believer had told some friends he wanted to start a café where people could obtain Bibles and discuss ideas, but other Christians told him, "You can't do that!"

When asked what they would do if they had religious freedom, some respondents said, "I would sing loudly."[16] Other answers included "Maybe some of us would get involved in politics," that they would start a school and "put a cross up in the school" or that they would "get on television."

Saving money for and providing for children is among the most compelling reasons for most people to accumulate wealth. Interviewees who had children were not optimistic that their Christian kids would be able to obtain a good education or jobs. They were torn between wanting their children to leave for a more welcoming environment or to stay and impact the next generation of Moroccans. One parent

---

[14] Gill and Shah, "Religious Freedom," 4.
[15] Although workplace discrimination against religion is illegal, interviewees said that co-workers and employers sometimes violate this principle with impunity or under circumstances where the violation would be hard to prove.
[16] Christ-followers must close their windows even on hot days if they don't wish to hear the ubiquitous calls to prayer. House church members sing softly to avoid reprimands or inquiries from neighbors and police. They love to take car trips and sing at the top of their lungs because no one can hear them there.

said, "For sure they grow in fear and are careful not to reveal their faith to others." But other parents said their children were openly identifying as Christians. One respondent with adult children said her son had been found with Christian materials in his car, and that the police said it was acceptable to possess them but not to sell or give them to anyone; he does so anyway. Another said that the younger generation of Christians "is less afraid but also less forgiving,"[17] holding the view that freedom is their inherent right. Two reported that teenagers had taken lunch to a park and eaten openly during the Ramadan fast (although it is technically illegal to do so), without reprisals.

Marriage, especially in the Islamic context, is intended to produce children and stimulate economic activity, also stabilizing the lives of young people. (Spend an evening watching Moroccan television and you will rarely see a young couple portrayed in commercials or music videos unless one or two children are playing at their knees.) One young man, who said he had been "a Muslim extremist" before his conversion, confided that he wanted to marry but could never do so because the marriage certificate begins, "In the name of Allah, in the name of Muhammad" and he refused "to sign anything in the name of Muhammad."

Another man had been waiting for over a year for his marriage license to be granted so that he could marry a Christian woman. He stated that he was not attending church while his application was under scrutiny. Other young adults said it is hard to find marriage prospects within the Christian community, due to restrictions on meetings and the danger of openly identifying with Jesus. Marriage does not guarantee economic stimulus, but it fosters economic stability for a couple and is predictive of productivity for their children. Marriage contributes to economic development by letting couples share fixed costs and allocate obligations efficiently, and by encouraging saving and other responsible behaviors.

3.2 Growth-promoting ideas

Gill and Shah suggest that to the extent that religious ideas are growth-promoting ideas, religious freedom will encourage healthy economies.[18] Honesty, as it is valuable for success in business and for escaping poverty, is doubtless a growth-promoting virtue. Morocco rated 39th of 40 countries in honesty in a study measuring that trait on the basis of how many planted "lost" wallets were returned to research

---

[17] One family insisted on giving their child a name not on the government-approved list of Muslim names; they held out for a name that appears only in the New Testament. After several months, the name was finally allowed, with no explanation.

[18] Gill and Shah, "Religious Freedom," 8–11. Anthony Gill, in "Religious Liberty and Economic Development: Exploring the Causal Connections," *Review of Faith and International Affairs* 11(4), Winter 2013, 12, is more tentative, but he is not addressing a particular religious idea there.

investigators.[19] Christianity enjoins truth telling and personal integrity (and nations historically steeped in Reformed Christianity topped the list of wallet returners in the aforementioned experiment, as well as consistently heading lists of economic prosperity).[20] Without implying any comment on what Islam teaches on this subject, not only is Morocco missing the added influence of Christianity's emphasis on honest dealings, but the suppression of religious freedom tempts persecuted people to engage in duplicity, bribery and crime. It also exposes the majority group to temptations of false accusation, nepotism and rigid thinking, all of which tend to be impediments to economic development.

Related to this problem, lack of interpersonal trust obstructs innovation, engagement in business, and involvement in complex, ambitious projects of all kinds.[21] Of the 32 people surveyed, 23 said it was hard to make long-term plans or that they had no "clear vision" of the future. One man said, "We are very few and fear to enter into business relations with other people." Another said of church members, "Many suffer silently," and "The street is for Muslims," indicating lack of access for Christians. Two parents said their children did not want to play with Muslim children because the Muslims tell them they are going to hell and ridicule or otherwise bully them; this divisive dynamic estranges Christian parents from their Muslim peers. Eight people indicated that they moved frequently to avoid detection or to escape the consequences of practicing their faith. Twelve said they were looking for chances to get out of Morocco. Although this question was not asked in the survey, two persons volunteered that they had no savings and no insurance; it appears that many followers of Jesus are in that situation.

A 10-year-old from a Christian family was recently asked whether he wanted to stay in Morocco or leave. He said, "I want to go out." He explained that he didn't want to be surrounded by Muslims because they are unkind to him; his schoolmates and teachers know he is a Christian and the teachers say he is condemned by Allah and make him memorize the Koran. Most parents of Christians would want their children to avoid being subjected to the Islamic education mandated by government schools. This attitude is in contrast to that of other Moroccan families,

---

[19] Kawtar Ennaji, "Global Honesty Index: Morocco at Bottom of the List," *Morocco World News,* 21 June 2019, https://www.moroccoworldnews.com/2019/06/276456/global-honesty-index-moroccans/amp/; Stephanie DeMarco, "Experiment with Lost Wallets," *Los Angeles Times,* 20 June 2019, https://www.latimes.com/science/la-sci-people-are-honest-lost-wallets-experiment-20190620-story.html, Figure 1.

[20] Peter L. Berger, "Max Weber Is Alive and Well," *Review of Faith and International Affairs* 8 (25 November 2010), https://doi.org/10.1080/15570274.2010.528964.

[21] Francis Fukuyama, *Trust: The Social Virtues and the Creation of Prosperity* (New York: Free Press, 1995), 29–30; Gill and Shah, "Religious Freedom," 26.

who may tend to think that the schooling is fine even if they believe that Europe may offer more possibilities for their grown children.

With regard to their attitude towards their surrounding society, one of the most common comments from the Christians surveyed was "We just want to be friends." This observation came from both new converts and more seasoned believers. This attitude reduces violence,[22] promotes social cohesion and aids the stability of institutions;[23] all these factors in turn support productive business activity. Several persons said their churches were trying to instill forgiving attitudes of "blessing your enemies" in their youngsters.

One recent convert said that when he told his wife he had become a Christian, she replied, "I will have to divorce you, then, because I'm a Muslim." He answered, "I told her, 'No, I don't want a divorce! I *love* you!'" Within a few weeks, she and other family members, seeing the positive changes in the man, had converted as well.

The Protestant work ethic, which comprises hard work and self-discipline, has been recognized as contributing to societal flourishing.[24] Two respondents said that whether they have religious freedom or not, they will "work hard." One man said he works every Friday so that his co-workers can go to the mosque. A few of those surveyed reported working on Sundays even when co-workers didn't, so that their families or colleagues would not suspect them of being at church. Unfortunately, working hard isn't always possible because some church members are unemployed or underemployed.

3.3 Charitable giving

Shah and Gill note that sometimes religious groups "mobilize their donations and volunteers to organize social services in a way that is more efficient than other entities, such as the state, or they provide services other institutions are unable or unwilling to provide."[25] In Morocco, the people interviewed were engaging in some of this activity, primarily by giving financial help to other believers who had been fired for converting to Christianity or who had had to leave home due to rejection by their families. Two other people, not part of the survey, are assisting various women who became pregnant out of wedlock.[26] According to these two helpers,

---

[22] Chris Seiple, "From Paradox to Possibility," *Review of Faith and International Affairs* 12(3), July 2014, 55–62, doi:10.1080/15570274.2014.943611.

[23] Daniel Philpott, "Religious Freedom and Peacebuilding: May I Introduce You Two?" *Review of Faith and International Affairs* 11(1), 2013, 31–37, https://doi-org.oralroberts.idm.oclc.org/10.1080/15570 274.2012.760977.

[24] Gill and Shah, "Religious Freedom," 8–9; Berger, "Max Weber."

[25] Gill and Shah, "Religious Freedom," 15–16.

[26] One of these two was not included in the survey because she still identifies as a Muslim, but she stated

such women supposedly don't exist in Muslim society. In extreme situations, they are either killed or forced to have abortions; sometimes they are sent "to the mountains" and usually live in obscurity thereafter.

In the survey, 11 respondents said that if they were free to do so, they would "help the poor" or do "social work" of some kind, and nine stated that they would offer classes in an existing setting or open a school or adult educational center. One said, "I could go back to my village and teach about health." Most said their church gives financial aid to members in need, but none said there was an organized program among Christians for that purpose.

3.4 Migratory magnet

Since the survey was initiated, two participating families have sent their children to European countries to begin college or career training. None have entered college in Morocco. As Shah and Gill observe, "To the extent that intelligent, entrepreneurial, and hard-working individuals are drawn to a society and expand its productivity by making more efficient use of its resources, they will enhance economic development and growth. ... This is true not only in terms of attracting migrants to settle in a territory but also in attracting merchants with whom to trade."[27] While in the United States, I spoke with an American Christian businessman, encouraging him to expand his franchise to Morocco; he expressed hesitancy, saying he did not want to do business where people of his religion might not succeed as franchisees. One skilled Moroccan Christian translator, newly married and a speaker of four languages, was hoping to leave the country because he wanted his children to be born in the United States. Although these are only anecdotal reports, they offer disheartening echoes of Gill and Shah's broad predictions.

3.5 Networks and voluntary associations

In Gill and Shah's paradigm, "The freedom of religious association contributes to social capital in terms of social networks and social trust, which can facilitate economic exchange and reduce corruption, and, in turn, promote economic growth."[28] As A. J. Conyers said, a healthy society is made of "myriad interlocking and overlapping groups ... of families, friendships, voluntary associations ... passing on obligations, intervening in disputes, distributing knowledge ... and providing a culture for the mutual expression of love and loyalty."[29] Churches and religious associa-

---

that she had a vision of the Virgin Mary, who urged her to do this kind of work. The other was living in another Muslim country at the time of the survey.

[27] Gill and Shah, "Religious Freedom," 18.

[28] Gill and Shah, "Religious Freedom," 28.

[29] A. J. Conyers, *The Long Truce* (Dallas, TX: Spence Publishing, 2001), 61, 85, 212, 243.

tions can perform these functions, increasing "social capital and a higher density of groups in civil society," in Gill and Shah's words.[30]

Ironically, several followers of Christ in Morocco have at least as many professional associations with Westerners as the average Muslim Moroccan has, because Christian Americans and Europeans sometimes seek them out as business contacts. One man works for a Western importer; another performs translation and research for a Spanish media company. One pastor communicates by Skype with an American Bible scholar on a weekly basis; another pastor hosted a youth leader from the Eastern United States to enhance his church's outreach to teens. If these people could pursue such opportunities openly, more international partnerships would develop.

In 2010, Morocco's High Council of Ulema, which comprises 7,000 Muslim leaders, declared Christian evangelism to be "moral rape" and "religious terrorism," backing up this judgement with a crackdown and confiscations of Christians' property.[31] When a religious minority undergoes discrimination, it tends to scatter for self-protection. Sixteen of our respondents mentioned that Christians were meeting in smaller groups than in the past, and in one city they have stopped meeting entirely. Two mentioned taking longer than previously to include a new person in religious activities, along with changing meeting places from time to time. One woman kept her children away from Bible camp for two years because police had questioned her about their activity. Some parents even leave their children at home while they attend house churches, to avoid making noise in the house church location that might attract attention, or to avoid subjecting their children to suspicion if the children repeat what they hear at worship.

3.6 Civil skills

Gill and Shah note that "religious adherents gain skills that are transferable to the secular economy and polity,"[32] such as organizing events, recruiting and serving as volunteers, caring for pooled resources, persuading others of their beliefs, research and resolving conflicts within their group.

I have met three Moroccan believers who have started "associations," or nonprofits that contribute to civil society. One was seeking to impart job skills to poor women in a small town, and another offered academic help to urban teenagers. One of these associations has since been closed by the government, and the founder believes that the closure was due to suspicions that the owner was Christian, though no official reason was given.

---

[30] Gill and Shah, "Religious Freedom," 26.

[31] Marshall, Gilbert, and Shea, *Persecution*.

[32] Gill and Shah, "Religious Freedom," 13.

Within the churches themselves, I have observed members planning events, organizing meals and recreation for 40 or more people, translating materials and working with a production studio to create and post materials about Christian character. I have also seen them do smaller things like creating a Facebook page for their church, arranging transportation for children from other towns to attend a Bible camp, and preparing song sheets and visuals for worship, along with grander undertakings such as setting up a meeting of 16 indigenous pastors to plan a national identity and network or even establishing an underground Bible school. Planning all-church events and establishing associations require not just organizational skills, but diplomacy and knowledge of the law, since these events are often interrupted by police asking questions about the event and who is involved. Because of the solidarity among members, they work together to help those who have lost a job, have been kicked out of the house due to conversion, or are facing a health crisis.

Thus, religious organizations can "serve as low-cost schools for individuals to develop economically and politically useful habits and skills."[33] As Hoover and Farr say of Pentecostalism, religious activity "teaches ordinary people to create and run their own grassroots institutions."[34]

Although Moroccan Christians are functioning in some of these ways, they are not allowed to participate fully in the cohesive Muslim society that surrounds them. Nor are they able to model for the children important skills needed for business success, such as innovation, proactive personality, generalized self-efficacy and autonomy.[35]

4. Conclusion

When people are unable to make long-term plans, form a variety of trusting relationships, count on the rule of law, sense a locus of control within themselves, or escape from constant, menacing scrutiny, they have little opportunity to contribute to their broader society. Morocco will be more prosperous when all of its people – including religious minorities – are free to flourish.

---

[33] Gill and Shah, "Religious Freedom," 12–13.

[34] Dennis R. Hoover and Thomas F. Farr, "In Search of the Bottom Line on Religious Freedom: An Introduction to the Winter 2013 Issue," citing Peter Berger, "Max Weber Is Alive and Well, and Living in Guatemala: The Protestant Ethic Today," *Review of Faith and International Affairs* 8(4): 3–9, doi: 10.1 080/15570274.2010.528964.

[35] Hermann Brandstatter, "Personality Aspects of Entrepreneurship: A Look at Five Meta-Analyses," *Personality and Individual Differences* 51(3), August 2011, 222–230, http://www.sciencedirect.com/ science/article/pii/S0191886910003454.

Invited but not welcomed
Where is the promised accommodation of separatist religious communities in Canada?

Janet Epp Buckingham[1]

Abstract

Canada is generally viewed as a country that respects human rights, but groups that maintain separation from society as part of their religious practices offer particular challenges with regard to protecting their religious freedom. This paper examines three separatist Anabaptist minorities in Canada – the Amish, Hutterites and Mennonites – and their history of religious accommodation. Often, the national government promised these groups accommodation to encourage them to immigrate to Canada, but provincial or local governments subsequently sought to undermine these accommodations. As a result, these groups have sometimes been excluded rather than welcomed.

Keywords   Anabaptist, religious minorities, accommodation, human rights, Canadian history.

1. Introduction

Canada is a multi-faith, multi-ethnic country that has traditionally welcomed groups persecuted in other countries. At least, this is part of the national myth. But it has not always been the case in practice. This paper looks at the experiences of three Anabaptist Christian communities – the Amish, Hutterites and some Mennonites – that have a strong view of the church's need for clear separation from society, which they perceive as worldly and evil.

Some of these groups were encouraged to immigrate to Canada with promises of accommodation of their specific religious needs. Provincial and local governments, however, have reversed some of these accommodations, and some separatist religious minority communities have had to fight court battles in an effort to maintain the freedom to practice their faith. Moreover, even the Canadian courts have not always been sympathetic to these minorities' peculiar religious practices.

---

[1]   Dr. Janet Epp Buckingham serves as a professor at Trinity Western University and director of the Laurentian Leadership Centre in Ottawa, Canada (www.twu.ca/llc). She previously served as legal counsel to the Evangelical Fellowship of Canada and as a representative of the World Evangelical Alliance at the United Nations. She received her LL.D. from the University of Stellenbosch, South Africa. Article received: 12 June 2019; accepted: 26 August 2019. Email: janet.epp-buckingham@twu.ca.

Richard Niebuhr identified five typologies concerning how Christians inter-
act with the surrounding culture in his seminal 1951 book *Christ and Culture*.
At the two ends of the spectrum are separatism and assimilation. Separatist
communities believe that the surrounding culture is evil and that Christians
must keep themselves as separate as possible to avoid sin. To achieve this goal,
separatists tend to build a strong, self-sufficient culture within their religious
communities and minimize interaction with and accommodation to the surrounding world.

At the opposite end of the spectrum, assimilationists see the surrounding culture
not as evil but rather as conducive to practicing the Christian faith. Between these
two extremes are dualists, synthesists and conversionists. These three moderate
approaches to Christ and culture allow believers to live with varying degrees of accommodation to their surrounding culture.

The separatist Anabaptist groups who now live in Canada trace their history
back to the Reformation in Switzerland in 1525. Although the three groups differ in organizational structure, dress, languages and modes of transportation, they
share certain core beliefs. "Like all Anabaptists, these beliefs include adult baptism,
the rigid separation of church and state, and the establishment of the church as a
Christian *community* that follows Jesus in all areas of life." (Hamilton 2007:160;
emphasis added) Beyond these core beliefs, each of these Anabaptist traditions
includes a range of beliefs and practices.

All these groups "locate moral authority in the community … and not in the individual" (Steiner 2015:25). Donald Kraybill and Carl Bowman, who refer to these
separatist groups as Old Order, explain further: "For them, such authority emerges
from *traditional practice*, rests on *collective wisdom*, and covers a *broad scope* of
behavior" (Kraybill and Bowman 2001:15). The opportunity to live in communities
is therefore an important requirement for these religious minorities. On Niebuhr's
typology, they are clearly separatists. They often separate themselves geographically
from mainstream culture and may wear distinctive clothing. Their separation from
society is an integral part of their religious beliefs and practices. All these groups
have faced considerable persecution and, as a result, have a long history of migra-
tions in search of a country or place where they could practise their communal,
separatist lifestyles in peace.

This paper examines the ways in which Canadian governments and courts have
addressed a variety of issues requiring accommodation for separatist Anabaptist
groups in Canada. After examining the promises made to these groups when they
immigrated to Canada, I then discuss how the promises were frequently broken.
In many cases, the national government made promises but provincial and local
governments subsequently sought to undermine the promised accommodations.

2. How the Canadian government system functions

How could the national government make promises to separatist communities, only to have provincial governments effectively gut them? Canada operates under a federal system of government. The national government has robust powers but cannot legislate in areas of provincial responsibility (Canada 1867:ss. 91–92). Education and healthcare fall under provincial jurisdiction, whereas the national government is responsible for immigration, foreign affairs, defence and criminal law. This distinction is important because, sometimes years or even decades after the national government made commitments to religious minorities to encourage them to immigrate to Canada, provincial or local governments not bound by those commitments adopted laws or policies that sought to force religious minorities to assimilate.

In 1982, Canada adopted a Charter of Rights and Freedoms. Section 2(a) of this Charter guarantees freedom of "conscience and religion." The Charter applies to laws and government policies and actions made by any level of government, whether national, provincial or municipal. Any law that violates religious freedom can be struck down or the courts can grant an appropriate remedy. As with many human rights documents, the rights guaranteed are subject to a limitation clause; that is, governments may limit rights under certain circumstances.

3. Three examples of 'separated communities' and their treatment by Canadian governments

3.1 Old Order Mennonites and Old Order Amish in Ontario

The Old Order Mennonites and Old Order Amish appear very similar to each other, but they differ in their historical and geographical development. The Amish split from the Mennonite/Swiss Brethren in 1693 over theological issues (Steiner 2015:27). The Old Order Amish broke away from the wider Amish community in the 1890s, largely over whether to worship in homes (the Old Order's preference) or meetinghouses (Steiner 2015:154).

Old Order Mennonites separated from the Mennonite Church in Canada in 1889 (Steiner 2015:150–151). The issue in this instance was modernization, including such practices as holding religious services in English and having Sunday School. The Old Order Mennonites maintained German as their language of worship and eschewed modernization in other areas of life. Members of both the Old Order Amish and Old Order Mennonites hold their property privately but locate close to one another.

Old Order Amish immigrated to Canada in the 1820s and settled in Wellesley and Mornington Townships in the province of Ontario. To this day, many continue to use horses and buggies for transportation and therefore require accommodations in road access and signage. In the 1996 case *Mornington (Township) v. Kuepfer,* several Old Order Amish from the hamlet of Newton were charged with keeping a horse in a barn contrary to the township's by-laws. A Justice of the Peace ruled that the by-law violated section 2(a) of the Charter of Rights and Freedoms, based on evidence of the importance of horses for transportation for the Old Order Amish, so they were not convicted.

Another more recent case shows the challenge Old Order Amish farmers face due to regulations intended to deal with modern agricultural realities. In *Stoll v. Kawartha Lakes (City) Committee of Adjustment* (2004), an Old Order Amish farmer sought permission to build a second house on his land for his daughter and her family. However, the official plan for the municipality did not allow a farm smaller than 200 acres in size to be severed. The purpose of the municipal law was to ensure that farms remained viable, but it assumed that farmers would use modern mechanical methods. The farmer failed to gain approval for the land division from the municipality and appealed to the Ontario Municipal Board, which granted the application in 2004. His argument was that if one was using Old Order Amish intensive farming techniques and no modern equipment, a farm almost 200 acres in size was too large. The Municipal Board considered that the farm was being operated in Old Order Amish style and would not be permanently severed, so it allowed Mr. Stoll to build another house on the property. It did not specifically consider the question of freedom of religion.

In these cases, although local municipalities made rules based on the practices of the majority population, courts were willing to override them to accommodate Old Order Mennonite and Old Order Amish populations.

3.2 Western Canadian Mennonites

The Canadian government encouraged German-speaking Mennonites to emigrate from Russia in the 1870s by negotiating accommodations to meet their religious requirements. John Lowe, Secretary of the Department of Agriculture, wrote a letter to the Mennonites promising exemption from military service, a reserve of eight townships in Manitoba for the settlement (since the Mennonites wanted to live in communities), the privilege of educating their children as they saw fit, and the ability to make affirmations rather than taking oaths (Epp 1974:338). With respect to education, the letter read, "The fullest privilege of exercising their religious principles is by law afforded without any kind of molestation or restriction whatever; and the same privilege extends to the education of their children in schools." The Department of Agriculture was responsible for immigration at that time. Seven thousand Mennonites immigrated to Manitoba on the basis of these commitments (Ens 1994:21).

However, the actual government policy approved by the Canadian Privy Council, the official advisory body to the Queen, in 1873 changed the wording of the commitment regarding education. The Council's order read, "That the Mennonites will have the fullest privilege of exercising their religious principles, and educating their children in schools, *as provided by law*, without any kind of molestation or restriction whatever" (Canada 1873; emphasis added). That change allowed the government to remove the Mennonites' right to religious education. It was not made public until 1916, however, and the Mennonites relied on John Lowe's letter as proof of their rights.

Although many practical problems arose from the settlement of German-speaking Mennonites from Russia in Manitoba, the Canadian government was willing to negotiate resolution of the difficulties so that immigration by members of this minority group would continue. The most significant concession concerned the allotment of land. Under the Canadian settlement system, called homesteading, settlers were entitled to a land grant of 160 acres if they built a house, cleared a certain amount of land, and lived on the property for three years (Canada 1872:s. 33(11)). In Russia, the Mennonites lived in villages and farmed the surrounding land. When they settled in Canada, they wanted to adopt the same manner of living (Epp 1974:212). Therefore, they would not qualify for homestead grants because they did not live on the homestead property. The Canadian government amended the Dominion Lands Act in 1876, allowing the Minister of the Interior to waive the residency requirement. This provision, which became known as the Hamlet Privilege, allowed the Russian Mennonites to continue their communal way of life (Ens 1994:36).

Between 1916 and 1919, provincial governments in Manitoba and Saskatchewan "sought to use the schools to inculcate patriotic sentiments and to foster Canadian nationalism" (Epp 1982:97). In 1916 and 1917, respectively, Manitoba and Saskatchewan passed changes to their education legislation, requiring that English be the language of instruction and making school attendance compulsory. Public schools were built and staffed in Mennonite villages that previously had only private Mennonite schools. The new public schools either had English names or were named for significant battles in the First World War; the latter practice was clearly insulting to pacifist Mennonites. Some of the schools were even staffed by teachers who were war veterans (Ens 1994:124–138). Nevertheless, under the new law Mennonites were obligated to send their children to the new public schools.

In 1918, both Manitoba and Saskatchewan governments began to prosecute Mennonites for failing to send their children to public schools, even though the children were attending local private schools. Mennonite parents were fined and jailed and had their property confiscated (Ens 1994:138–146). In one of these prosecutions, *R. v. Hildebrand and Doerksen*, the parents challenged the validity of the provincial law, raising the national government guarantee. In that case, the Manitoba Court of Appeal ruled in 1919 that the provincial government had exclusive jurisdiction over education and that the national government could not guarantee educational rights in the province. The John Lowe letter on which Mennonites had relied was declared not valid with respect to education, as it was superseded by the order of the Canadian Privy Council.

When it became clear to the Mennonites that Manitoba and Saskatchewan would no longer allow them to educate their own children and that the national government would not intervene on their behalf, they looked to emigrate. Some 6,000 Mennonites relocated from Canada to Latin America, mostly Mexico and Paraguay, in the 1920s (Janzen 1990:98) These separatist Mennonites made considerable financial sacrifices to live by their religious principles (Epp 1982:119–124).

Ironically, at the same time as some Mennonites were leaving Western Canada for Latin America, more German-speaking Mennonites in Russia sought to immigrate to Canada as they faced persecution after the Bolshevik revolution (Epp 1982:146). However, by then the Canadian government had adopted its 1919 Immigration Act, including a provision specifically designed to prohibit the immigration of Mennonites and Hutterites. Mennonites in Canada advocated strenuously for Canada to accept these new separatist believers as immigrants. After several years of negotiation, including negotiations between Canadian and Russian government officials, Canada allowed some 20,000 German-speaking Mennonites from Russia to enter the country between 1923 and 1930 (Epp 1982:152–179).

3.3 The Hutterian Brethren

Jonnette Watson Hamilton notes:

> From their very beginnings, the Hutterites' religious beliefs and practices have challenged the values and authority of the established state. Their history of relations with their host nations has therefore been one of broken promises, persecution and flight. (Hamilton 2007:161)

Hutterites are unique even amongst Anabaptist groups in their strong focus on close communal living. Their religious beliefs require that they hold property communally and live in 'colonies.' They have not been willing to compromise on this point. As Yossi Katz and John Lehr (2012:xi) point out, "The rural colony system is thus integral and vital to the practise of their faith." This unusual religious practice required that religious leaders negotiate with the government to ensure that they could get exemptions from typical landholding systems and that they could operate schools on Hutterite colonies that only Hutterite children would be permitted to attend.

Law professor Alvin Esau describes a Hutterite colony's self-perception as an "ark of salvation that leads to eternal life in heaven, while the rest of the world is drowning in the flood of temporary selfish pride and pleasure leading to death" (Esau 2004:x). This is an allusion to the biblical story of Noah and the ark, according to which the world was flooded because of sin and only Noah's family and the animals on the ark survived.

Hutterites began to emigrate from the United States to Canada after the First World War because they faced persecution due to their refusal to serve in the military. The sect originated in Eastern Europe and, like the Mennonites, migrated to Russia due to persecution. When Russia restricted exemption from military service, Hutterites immigrated to the United States. The above-noted prohibition on Hutterite immigration to Canada was lifted in the late 1920s.

During the Second World War, the Hutterites were quite unpopular in Alberta due to their pacifism. In 1942, the Alberta government passed the Land Sales Prohibition Act, which prohibited the sale of land to "any enemy alien or Hutterite." After the war, this law was changed to the Alberta Communal Property Act (Alberta 1947; Janzen 1990:68–73) which replaced the outright ban with restrictions on the size of colonies, their proximity to one another and the amount of land Hutterites could own in any one county. But given their high birth rate, Hutterite colonies needed to be able to found nearby daughter colonies on a regular basis. Accordingly, the Hutterites filed a constitutional challenge against this discriminatory law, *Hatch v. East Cardston Colony*, which was decided in 1949. Their legal action was not successful, as the judge ruled that he did not have the jurisdiction to consider the constitutionality of the legislation.

The Alberta law was amended again in 1950 (in An Act to Amend the Communal Property Act, s. 1) to further restrict Hutterite colonies by requiring provincial cabinet approval for any new colony to be established. According to Hamilton (2007:167), however, the Hutterites found ways to "evade the restrictions when it became too difficult to acquire adequate land to sustain their way of life." The Alberta government appointed the Hutterite Investigation Committee in 1958 and further changes were made, with the ultimate goal of achieving assimilation of the Hutterites (Hamilton 2007:167–168).

A second constitutional challenge, *Walter v. A.G. of Alberta*, was appealed all the way to the Supreme Court of Canada, which upheld the law in 1969. This time the applicants asked for a declaration that the law was beyond the legislative authority of the provincial government for the provincial government on the basis of three arguments: first, the legislation related primarily to religion; second, it was discriminatory and breached national government assurances made when the Hutterites immigrated to Canada; and third, it contravened the protections of religious freedom contained in the 1960 Canadian Bill of Rights. The Supreme Court ruled, however, that the Act was within provincial jurisdiction since it governed property.

The Communal Property Act was finally repealed in 1972, on the basis that it violated human rights (Katz and Lehr 2012:147). The province of Alberta passed its own bill of rights and the Individual Rights Protection Act in that same year. A Hutterite Liaison Office was established to work with a Hutterite Committee of Elders on developing guidelines for Hutterite land acquisitions (Hamilton 2007:177).

In Saskatchewan, municipalities passed by-laws to restrict the proliferation of colonies. However, in the 1979 case *R. v. Vanguard Hutterian Brethren*, a colony accused of violating a resolution by undertaking construction without a permit was exonerated. The problem was that the rural municipality involved had refused to grant a permit. Under Saskatchewan's Planning and Development Act, municipalities may give notice that they are preparing a by-law and require that all development that may be affected by the by-law be subject to written consent from the council until the by-law is passed, for up to one year following the notice. The rural municipality gave such notice but did not prepare a by-law within the subsequent year. Its behaviour constituted clear evidence that this manoeuvre was not in good faith but was intended to frustrate the Hutterite colony's attempts to locate in the municipality. Accordingly, the Saskatchewan Court of Queen's Bench dismissed the charge against the colony.

The province of Manitoba also placed restrictions on Hutterite colonies from 1957 to 1971. These restrictions were repealed as a result of a negotiated settlement between the Hutterites and the Union of Manitoba Municipalities. However, as late as 1982 the Union was still contemplating the possibility of making a formal request to the provincial government to reinstate restrictions (UPI 1982). By that time, the Charter of Rights and Freedoms had come into force and the provincial government said that such restrictions would violate the Charter.

The most recent issue relating to government treatment of Hutterites is the Alberta government's requirement (Operator Licensing and Vehicle Control Amendment, Regulation 137 of 2003) that all driver licences must contain a photograph of the driver. Some Hutterites object to having their photograph taken, believing that this would constitute a violation of Exodus 20:4, which prohibits the making of graven images. The colony sought to have the government's regulation declared invalid on the basis that it infringed upon the Hutterites' religious freedom, since they could not get a driver licence without violating a tenet of their religious beliefs. The Supreme Court of Canada ruled against the Hutterites in the 2009 decision *Alberta v. Hutterian Brethren of Wilson Colony*.

Chief Justice McLachlin, writing for the majority of the Supreme Court, ruled that there was indeed a violation of religious freedom. However, she considered that infringement justified by the significant objective underlying the requirement of photo identification, namely, protection against fraud and identity theft. She also found that the minimal impairment test was met; the law was proportional to the objective, there were no alternative ways to meet the government's objective of maintaining the integrity of the driver's licence system, and the government was not obligated to accommodate the Hutterites' religious practices.

Chief Justice McLachlin stated that the Hutterites could hire drivers if they did not want to have their photographs taken. This suggestion mischaracterizes the importance of the colony's separation from the rest of society. Hutterite colonies deliberately limit contact with the outside community (Koshan and Hamilton 2010:para. 7). At the time of the decision, colony members publicly discussed driving without licences (Komarnicki 2010) or emigrating from Alberta (White 2009).

Professor Richard Moon argues that, sadly, this decision is consistent with previous Supreme Court of Canada rulings: "The Court's adoption of this weak standard of justification under section 1 reflects an ambivalence about the nature of religious commitment and its place in the public life of the community" (Moon 2010:para. 66). As lawyer Marshall Haughey comments, "The decision in Wilson Colony marks another chapter in the struggle for Hutterian colonies to maintain their way of life" (Haughey 2011:para. 70).

4. Conclusions

At various times in Canada's history, the national government has actively encouraged separatist Anabaptist minority religious communities to relocate to Canada with promises of various accommodations for their communal and religious lifestyles. However, the national government has not 'practiced what they preached' but rather has allowed these promises to be undermined or even overridden by zealous provincial and municipal governments. In other situations, changing circumstances have made these separatist groups less popular. The groups have pursued legal action to protect their religious freedom, but the courts have usually been less than sympathetic.

Provincial governments have placed restrictions on the religious practices of separatist Anabaptist religious communities, pushing believers to conform, engage in civil disobedience or even emigrate from Canada in order to maintain their religious traditions and educate their children in what they considered an appropriate manner. Recently, the Supreme Court of Canada has failed to respect the Hutterites' religiously based need for an alternative to driver licences with photos, thereby creating hardship for Hutterite colonies.

Although the separatist religious communities described in this paper comprise very small populations in Canada, the lack of accommodation for their beliefs indicates the country's incomplete respect for religious difference. How countries accommodate minority religious communities whose religious practices diverge significantly from those of mainstream society is a bellwether for freedom of religion more generally. Canada has invited these religious communities to immigrate, but its subsequent treatment of them has been very cool. As a country that touts its commitment to inclusion and diversity, Canada can do better.

References

Alberta. 1942. *Land Sales Prohibition Act,* S.A. 1942, c. 16.

Alberta. 1947. *Alberta Communal Property Act,* S.A. 1947, c. 16.

Alberta. 1950. *An Act to amend the Communal Property Act,* S.A. 1950, c. 10.

Alberta. 1972. *Communal Property Repeal Act,* S.A. 1972, c. 103.

Alberta. 2003. *Operator Licensing and Vehicle Control Amendment Regulation,* Alta. Reg. 137/2003.

Alberta v. Hutterian Brethren of Wilson Colony. 2009. 2 Supreme Court Reports 567.

Canada. 1867. *Constitution Act, 1867,* 30 & 31 Vict., c. 3.

Canada. 1872. *Dominion Lands Act,* S.C. 1872, c. 23.

Canada. 1873. *Order-in-Council,* P.C. no 957, 13 August, NA, RG 2, 1, vol. 83.

Canada. 1876. S.C. 1876, c. 19.

Canada. 1919. *An Act to Amend the Immigration Act,* S.C. 1919, c. 25.

Canada. 1960. *Canadian Bill of Rights,* S.C. 1960, c. 44.

Canada. 1982. *Canadian Charter of Rights and Freedoms, The Constitution Act, 1982,* R.S.C. 1985, Appendix II, No. 44.

Canadian Privy Council. 1872. Orders-in-council, no. 1043D, 25 September 1872.

Ens, Adolf. 1994. *Subjects or Citizens? The Mennonite Experience in Canada, 1870–1925.* Ottawa: University of Ottawa Press.

Epp, Frank H. 1974. *Mennonites in Canada 1786–1920: The History of a Separate People.* Toronto: Macmillan.

Epp, Frank H. 1982. *Mennonites in Canada 1920–1940: A People's Struggle for Survival.* Toronto: Macmillan.

Esau, Alvin J. 2004. *The Courts and the Colonies: The Litigation of Hutterite Church Disputes.* Vancouver: UBC Press.

Hamilton, Jonnette Watson. 2007. Space for religion: Regulation of Hutterite expansion and the Superior Courts of Alberta, in *The Alberta Supreme Court at 100: History and authority,* edited by Jonathan Swainger. Edmonton: University of Alberta Press: 159–192.

Hatch v. East Cardston Colony. 1949. 1 Western Weekly Reports 900 (Alberta District Court).

Haughey, Marshall. 2011. The camera and the colony: A comment on *Alberta v. Hutterian Brethren of Wilson Colony. Saskatchewan Law Review* 74:59–82.

Janzen, William. 1990. *Limits on liberty: The experience of Mennonite, Hutterite, and Doukhobor communities in Canada.* Toronto: University of Toronto Press.

Katz, Yossi and Lehr, John. 2012. *Inside the ark: The Hutterites in Canada and the United States.* Regina: CPRC Press.

Komarnicki, Jamie. 2010. Hutterites may defy driving law. Calgary Herald, 28 February.

Koshan, Jennifer and Hamilton, Jonnette Watson. 2010. Terrorism or whatever: The implications of *Alberta v. Hutterian Brethren of Wilson Colony* for women's equality and social justice. *Supreme Court Law Review,* 2nd series, 50:221–256.

Kraybill, Donald B. and Bowman, Carl F. 2001. *On the backroad to heaven: Old Order Hutterites, Mennonites, Amish, and Brethren.* Baltimore: Johns Hopkins University Press.

Manitoba. 1890. *The Public Schools Act*, 53 Vict., c. 38.

Moon, Richard. 2010. Accommodation without compromise: Comment on *Alberta v. Hutterian Brethren of Wilson Colony. Supreme Court Law Reports,* 2nd series, 51:95–130.

Mornington (Township) v. Kuepfer. 1996. 1996 O.J. 1724.

Niebuhr, H. Richard. 1951. *Christ and Culture.* New York: Harper & Brothers.

R. v. Hildebrand and Doerksen. 1919. 3 Western Weekly Reports 286 (Manitoba Court of Appeal), leave to appeal to Privy Council refused.

R. v. Vanguard Hutterian Brethren. 1979. 6 Western Weekly Reports 335 (Saskatchewan District Court).

Re Jensen. 1976. 2 F.C. 665 (Citizenship App. Ct).

Saskatchewan. 1973. *Planning and Development Act,* S.S. 1973, c. 72.

Socknat, Thomas. 1987. *Witness against war: Pacifism in Canada, 1900–1945.* Toronto: University of Toronto Press.

Steiner, Samuel J. 2015. *In search of promised lands: A religious history of Mennonites in Ontario.* Kitchener: Herald Press.

Stoll v. Kawartha Lakes (City) Committee of Adjustment. 2004. O.M.B.D. No. 866.

UPI. 1982. Legislation restricting Hutterite land ownership would violate the Charter. 24 November. Available at https://www.upi.com/Archives/1982/11/24/Legislation-restricting-Hutterite-land-ownership-would-violate-the-Charter/4793406962000/.

Walter v. A.G. of Alberta. 1969. Supreme Court Reports 383.

White, Patrick. 2009. In wake of court ruling, Hutterites contemplate leaving Alberta. *The Globe and Mail,* 26 July, https://www.theglobeandmail.com/news/national/in-wake-of-court-ruling-hutterites-contemplate-leaving-alberta/article4280495/.

Thomas Schirrmacher

Human Rights

Promise and Reality

VKW   The WEA Global Issues Series 15

WEA
WORLD EVANGELICAL ALLIANCE

International Institute for Religious Freedom

IIRF

Historical roots of the manipulation of religion in Northern Nigeria

The rise of fundamentalist groups and the plight
of ethnic and religious minorities

Emmanuel Osewe Akubor[1]

Abstract

The manipulation of religion, especially by religious and political leaders, has plagued Nigeria ever since it gained its independence in 1960. The inability of the government and people to check this rising tide has led to religious violence in various parts of the country. This manipulation has led to the emergence of fundamentalist groups who are no longer interested in just creating internal crises but are currently working towards the disintegration of the country and the creation of a religious state. Thus, it is not surprising that the Boko Haram group, which made itself known in 2009, has taken over parts of the northern region. As a result, minorities in these occupied areas are often the target of attacks. These groups are frequently supported by powerful politicians and religious leaders pursuing their own selfish interests. This paper examines how the manipulation of religion in Nigeria since independence has fostered the rise of fundamentalist groups and describes the serious dangers facing minorities in the affected areas in particular and the nation of Nigeria in general.

Keywords: Religion, fundamentalism, religious minorities, Nigeria.

1. Introduction

Since the 1980s, religious crises have become a recurring part of life in northern Nigeria, affecting nearly every one of the 19 states that constitute this region. Some of the sources of the frustrations and criminal behaviour underlying these crises are clear: ethnic and religious division, sociological and economic alienation due to widespread poverty and unemployment. But other forces are involved whose identity and character are difficult to define.

Many people have died, sustained serious injuries, lost property, and/or become permanently dislocated and psychologically depressed as a result of these clashes, which pose a severe threat to public safety and citizens' rights. Furthermore, through either miscarriage of justice or the government's failures to prosecute the

---

[1]	Emmanuel Osewe Akubor teaches history at Obafemi Awolowo University, Ile-Ife, Osun State, Nigeria. Email: oseweakubor@gmail.com. Article received: 24 June 2015; accepted: 14 January 2020.

perpetrators and instigators of these clashes, thousands of Nigerians have been unjustly treated.

2. Intergroup relations before the emergence of Islam and Christianity

Although clashes between the two dominant world religions of Islam and Christianity have occurred periodically, there is no precedent in Nigeria for the type of skirmishes experienced today. This is because the various groups that inhabited the area traditionally viewed religion as a tool to promote unity, social stability and integration (Parrinder 1969; Kukah 2007).

Smith (1987, cited in Kwanashie et al., 1987) described the pre-Islamic Hausa land as a country of people who were dedicated to the worship of *Iskoki* (spirits), especially on the small mountains of Kano and Zaria. According to his analysis, the worship at these inselbergs provided fertile ground for the emergence of the society in which the jihadists later established Islam. In this way, Smith demonstrated that religion aided the substantial integration of people who came from different places to worship and later formed indivisible communities. In the southern part of Nigeria, before the arrival of Islam or Christianity, tribal religions cemented relationships and served as a tool for development. This is seen by the fact that worshippers of the different earth goddesses and priests and priestesses of similar deities had to come together to perform functions aimed at either purifying the land and its people, warning of impending danger or performing rituals to ask for a bountiful harvest (Afigbo, 1981).

3. Islam, Christianity and their co-existence in Nigeria since 1960

The socio-political situation in Nigeria since 1960 reminds one of the comment by Chief Awolowo, a post-colonial leader, that "Nigeria is a mere geographical expression." Nigeria's political independence was not gained with the full agreement and mutual satisfaction of all its regions. Bitterness persists even today in some parts of the country. Historical documents contain ample evidence of advocacy against, as well as in favour of, independence. Some areas saw considerable, open rejection of the call of independence, because of the fear that one region would dominate others. Such fears have proved to be well grounded. As François Duvalier, then president of Haiti, said in 1969, Nigeria has never since its independence shown the distinctive marks of a united nation. The country has been unable to quell tribal rivalries and achieve the cultural blending required to forge national unity (Onwudiwe 2011).

Duvalier's observation may have been based on his observation of the utterances and actions of Nigeria's political and religious leaders, who according to Usman (1979) were interested in religion only so that they could manipulate it for other purposes. Sir Ahmadu Bello (premier of Northern Nigeria until his assassination in 1966) and some other leaders gave the impression, in various settings, that the marriage that resulted in the country of Nigeria is unholy and must not be accepted (Paden, 1986). They have suggested that one religion or group is superior to the others and that, as such, the others should be perpetually enslaved and subservient. This negative perception of fellow citizens could also be partly responsible for the promotion of the present crises in the country.

4. The numbers game and heightened tensions

At various times in Nigeria's history, there has been debate over which religious population actually dominates the others. For example, in 1988, while reporting the riot that greeted the appointment of Ibrahim Dasuki as Sultan of Sokoto, the seat of the Caliphate in West Africa, both the British Broadcasting Corporation and the Voice of America described the Sultan as the spiritual head of the Muslims of Nigeria, who (they stated) consisted of 40% of the population. Within a week, letters and official condemnation of such a low reported percentage followed. The responses claimed that 70% to 80% of the population were Muslims.

Earlier, in 1986, Abubakar Gumi said that Nigeria was 80% Muslim, 5% Christian, and 15% others. When he received the King Faisal Prize in 1987, he claimed a 70% Muslim population for the country (IPA, 1989:16). In sharp contrast, Tijani Ibrahim (1989) argued that in Nigeria about 47% of the people were Muslims, 34% were Christians and 1% followed traditional religion. Recently it was claimed that there are 78 million Muslims in Nigeria, representing 5% of all Islamic adherents in the world (IPA, 1989:16). Usman Faruk, a former military governor of North-West state during General Yakubu Gowon's regime, argued (at Sheik Ahmad Gumi's Ramadan sermon at the Sultan Bello Mosque in Kaduna on 13 August 2012) that Nigeria had 120 million Muslims and only 50 million people of other faiths. These claims and counter-claims are all attempts at manipulating the people against one another. The immediate result has been the emergence of fundamentalist groups who have felt that the religion of the supposed majority should be forced on others.

5. The rise of fundamentalist groups and Nigeria's fragile unity: From Maitastine to Jama'atu Ahliss-Sunnah Lidda'awati Wal Jihad (Boko Haram)

5.1 The Maitatsine group

The Maitatsine group, named after the late Malam Muhammadu Marwa (also known as Allah Ta-Tsine or Maitatsine), initiated modern Nigeria's age of religious terrorism and fanaticism through the riots it fomented in the early 1980s (Yakub, 1992). Espousing an ideology that opposed most aspects of modernization and all

Western influence, the group unleashed acts of terrorism against the state. It also decried such technological commonplaces as radios, wrist watches, automobiles, motorcycles and even bicycles. Those who used these items or read books other than the Qur'an were viewed as hell-bound.

The first Maitatsine violence in Kano shocked many Nigerians to their marrow. In that crisis period, 4,177 lives were lost. The Kano incident stands out as the first Nigerian religious crisis to claim a huge toll in human lives and property. Although there had been a series of religious tensions and skirmishes across the country, including one in May 1980 in Zaria during which property belonging mainly to Christians was destroyed by some Muslims, the Maitatsine riots were at an unforeseen level. Most people could not imagine why differences in religion could lead to such wanton destruction of lives and property as occurred at Kano in December 1980 (Kumolu 2011).

The Maitatsine uprising has been described as the gateway to religious strife in Nigeria. Subsequent violent outbursts and religious riots have included the following:

➢ The Maitatsine uprising at Kano, Kaduna and Maiduguri in October 1982
➢ The Maitatsine uprising at Yola, February 1984
➢ The Maitatsine uprising at Gombe, April 1985
➢ The conflict in Kafanchan, Kaduna, Zaria and parts of Kaduna state, March 1987
➢ The conflict in Tafawa Balewa and other parts of Bauchi state in 1991, and again in 2000–2001
➢ The conflicts in Zango Kataf and other parts of Kaduna state from February to May 1992
➢ The conflicts in Kano state in 1999–2000
➢ The conflict in the Kaduna metropolis in 2000
➢ The Kano "Anti-American war in Afghanistan" riot of September–October 2001
➢ The *Sharia Dole* (Sharia is compulsory) conflict of 18 June 2001
➢ The conflict in the Jos metropolis and its environs in 2001–2002
➢ The conflict on the Mambila Plateau in 2001–2002
➢ The conflict in Gwantu, Kaduna state in 2001
➢ The Anti–Miss World conflict in Kaduna state, 2002–2003
➢ The Jos crisis/religious conflicts of November 2008 and 2010
➢ The Boko Haram uprising in Maiduguri and Bauchi, 2009
➢ The Kalakatu religious conflict in Bauchi, 2009

5.2 Jama'atu Ahliss-Sunnah Lidda'awati Wal Jihad (Boko Haram) and the Nigerian State

Jama'atu Ahliss-Sunnah Lidda'awati Wal Jihad, also known as Boko Haram (meaning "Western education is a sin"), is a Salafist Muslim sect that was founded around

2002 and became jihadist in 2009. It rejects Western education and forbids its members from working in any government establishment. The name Boko Haram may have been given to the group by members of the Hausa-speaking public because of its prominent opposition to Western education (Akubor, 2011). This organization also promotes separatism based on ethnic and sectarian intolerance, and it is the leading proponent of terror in Nigeria today. The original name is an Arabic phrase meaning "Group Committed to Propagating the Prophet's Teachings and Jihad." The group, originally based in the northeastern part of Nigeria, has spread its wings to other areas, especially the northwest, threatening the peace and stability of the entire country.

At its inception, Boko Haram was involved mostly in fomenting sectarian violence. Its adherents participated in simple attacks on Christians using clubs, machetes and small arms. The group gained international attention following a serious outbreak of inter-communal violence in 2008 and 2009 that resulted in thousands of deaths. Since that time, Boko Haram has continually attacked those who oppose its teachings and doctrines. Table 1 summarizes the attacks mounted in 2011 and 2012 in detail, with general reference to the ongoing violence Boko Haram has sustained since then.

A critical analysis of the modus operandi of the fundamentalist groups and their related allies shows clearly that they are on a genocide mission. A group bent on genocide, like the Hutus of Rwanda in their genocide against the Tutsis, starts by identifying the ethnic or national group they wish to annihilate. Then they use media propaganda effectively to arouse hatred against this target group. The propaganda helps in brainwashing militant youth, who are organized into militia to exterminate the target group. Taking control of the national or ethnic group whose fanatical militants are being prepared to perpetuate genocide also entails the elimination of rational and liberal members of that group who are opposed to genocide. They are called traitors from within, as the militants generate extreme tension, crisis and fear within both the target group and their own group. In most cases, they capitalize on a serious national crisis – economic or political – to unleash their violence on innocent people. In doing so, those who are placed in strategic state institutions use those institutions, whether national or local, to assist in the implementation of their genocide (Destexhe 1995; Prunier 1995).

6. The politics of the widening Christian-Muslim divide since 1999

Maier (2000) argued that the relationship between Nigerian Christians and Muslims took a devastating turn with the return of democracy in 1999, when several northern governors openly called for the imposition of the complete Islamic legal system known as Sharia, including its penalties of amputation and floggings and its strict code

	Date	Target	Implement	Result
1	26 Aug. 2011	UN headquarters, Abuja	Suicide bomber	Scores killed and UN building destroyed
2	22 Sept. 2011	Mandala, Niger State	Unknown	Five Igbo traders killed for inability to recite Qur'an
3	4 Nov. 2011	Maiduguri, Potiskum and Kaduna	Explosives, guns and suicide bomber	Over 160 lives lost and properties destroyed
4	Dec. 2011	Oriapkata, Kaduna	Explosives	Scores injured and killed
5	12 Dec. 2011	Mando, Kaduna	Explosives	Scores injured, building destroyed
6	Dec. 2011	Yobe and Maiduguri	Explosives and raids	Policemen and others injured and killed
7	25 Dec. 2011	St Theresa Catholic Church, Mandalla, Niger State	Explosives	Worshippers and residents injured and killed
8	25 Dec. 2011	Yobe and Plateau states	Explosives	People killed
9	1 Jan. 2012	Winners Chapel, Sapele Road, Benin	Planted explosives	Foiled, suspects arrested
10	5 Jan. 2012	Deeper Life Church, Gombe	Guns (attack during worship inside church)	6 killed, 10 injured
11	5 Jan. 2012	Adamawa State	Gunmen	4 Christian/Igbo traders killed
12	6 Jan. 2012	Christ Apostolic Church, Jimeta Yola	Boko Haram gunmen	8 killed
13	6 Jan. 2012	Mubi, Adamawa State	Boko Haram gunmen	About 20 Igbo/Christians killed during a town hall meeting
14	6 Jan. 2012	Adamawa State	Boko Haram gunmen	Killed kinsmen of murdered Christians planning burial rites
15	7 Jan. 2012	University of Maiduguri	Boko Haram gunmen	2 Christian students killed
16	7 Jan. 2012	Larmurde, Adamawa	Boko Haram gunmen	7 Christians killed on their way out of Adamawa
17	22 Jan. 2012	St Theresa Catholic Church and Evangelical Church Tafawa Balewa	Explosives	No lives lost
18	29 April 2012	Bayero University Kano, Old Campus	Guns and explosives	Worshippers killed including students and 2 professors
19	2012–2015	Maiduguri and Yobe	Guns and explosives	Many people killed

Table 1: Attacks on People and Places by Boko Haram since 2011

of sexual segregation. They did so without taking into consideration the religious com-position of the area, which had Muslims and Christians living side by side.

Sharia was first implemented by the government of Zamfara state under Yerima Bakura, followed immediately by the government of Niger state and more than a dozen other northern states. Those who supported this movement told their Muslim supporters that living under the Sharia system is an intrinsic right and duty of the Islamic faithful, and that any Muslim who opposed it was lacking in true belief. On the other hand, Christians within these territories, as well as those Muslims who doubted the wisdom of pressing for Sharia, saw this effort as an attempt to undermine the Christians in the area. The argument that Sharia would not affect non-Muslims was seen as largely false; for example, the ban on the sale of alcohol, cinemas and integration of the sexes in most spheres of public life would affect everyone irrespective of religion and tribe. The resulting controversy set the people openly against each other, leading to hundreds of deaths and the burning and loot-ing of businesses in many areas of northern Nigeria (Maier 2000).

Yahaya (2007) corroborated Maier's reports, noting that the losses in monetary terms could have funded a substantial programme of development projects. He indicated that the bloody clash in Kaduna in the year 2000 not only led to a major breakdown of inter-group relations, but also claimed 1,295 lives and saw the de-struction of 1,944 buildings (including 123 churches and 55 mosques) and 746 vehicles. A large number of residents fled, making Kaduna seem like a ghost town for a long time and initiating the unplanned division of Kaduna metropolis into the Muslim north and Christian south.

In the midst of counter-attacks that led to an estimated 400 deaths of Muslims in the northern city of Aba, the Kano state government proceeded to enact the Sharia bill into law on 27 February 2000, just two days before an emergency meeting that the President had called to look into the matter. Several other states, includ-ing Yobe, Borno and Sokoto, were actively considering similar measures at this time. The Christian business communities in the north argued that these laws were intended to attack them and their businesses, and subsequent events seem to have confirmed their fears. For example, in March 2010 the Kano Hisbah (a religious police force) destroyed 34,000 bottles of confiscated alcohol. Kano state has also maintained steep fines and prison sentences for the public consumption and dis-tribution of alcohol, in compliance with its Sharia statutes. Hisbah has been ac-cused of harassing non-residents as well as non-Muslim residents of Kano state who were transporting alcoholic beverages on federal roads in Kano. Furthermore, on 1 March 2010, the Kano State Censorship Board cancelled a three-night interna-tional music festival that had been hosted by the French embassy for six consecutive years. They argued that the event included a musician who had previously spoken out against the board's censorship of certain music in Kano state (US Bureau of Democracy, Human Rights, and Labor, 2010). Some scholars have also objected to the use of state funds to support one religious group over others, because the state government constructed 75 Juma'a (Friday) and 65 hamsu-salawat (general) mosques between 2005 and 2006 (Haruna 2010) but did not construct a single building for a church or even for Christian interdenominational affairs.

7. Religious manipulation and the plight of northern minorities and other ethnic nationalities

Although Islam is widely practiced in northern Nigeria, the emergence of fundamentalist groups in this part of the country has led to major adulteration and manipulation of Islamic teaching, such that extreme views have gradually come to be seen as amongst the basic tenets of the religion. One impact of this evolution has been the oppression of those who have refused to accept these extreme teachings. The objectors have been marginalized in society and referred to as *Kaafir* (infidels) or *Maguzawa* (unbelievers). Whereas the term *Kaafir* (or *kufr* or *Kuffar*) is used to describe non-believers in Islam generally, *Maguzawa* is used for indigenous people who have refused to accept the Muslim religion and as such are viewed as infidels (Akubor and Musa 2018). The Kaafir are often left alone to live in their own separate area, so that they don't influence other people and their religious practice, but the Maguzawa face active discrimination politically, economically, socially and educationally. They have been denied official permission to build their own schools or to engage in other development activities due to their religious affiliation. These forms of discrimination and lack of opportunity appear to be part of a plan by a portion of the northern oligarchy to maintain control over minorities in the north (Akubor and Musa 2018). In other cases, educational institutions that were established by local residents or missionaries have been shut down (Kukah 2012). One school located in the Igabi Local Government Area of Kaduna state, which was predominantly a Christian community, was converted into an Islamic school and all the Christian students were sent home (Anfani 2001).

Religious minorities, especially the Maguzawa, have been intentionally denied job opportunities. Anfani (2001) provided the following example:

> In Kaduna State, an advertisement was placed for job vacancy where there were 54 spaces on the notice board in one of the ministries in Kaduna State. According to the source, even though the interview was done with lots of inconsistencies, only 38 names were listed as people who got the vacancies, of which only four were Christians from the southern part of Kaduna. From the northern part of Kaduna no single one who is a Christian was taken. … For example, in Kaduna State, when the

forms were sent to one local government chairman he said he has no Joshua, no Elijah and no Samuel [a reference to Christians and Christian names] in his local government so he will not sign it and up till today after making that report, only Kaduna State was purported to have received the forms. All other states have not received the forms. The same thing with the poverty alleviation program.

Land use rights have been a closely related issue. The Islamic fundamentalist groups still hold firmly to the colonial policy of divide-and-rule and the setting up of separate settlements for non-indigenes; in addition, indigenous members of the minority religion are continually being denied access to land. This was the case with the Tundun Wada and Sabongari settlements, to which indigenous people, displaced inhabitants of the city and non-indigenous immigrants subject to the native administration were restricted, while the ancient walled cities were meant for the indigenous Muslims (Akubor and Akinwale 2014:20). During the colonial period, this provision was intended to prevent people of other religions and ethnic nationalities from mixing freely with the indigenes, as the latter group was considered more radical and a 'bad influence.' Ibe (1998:5) argued that in this way, the colonial British approved of the subjugation of the northern minorities and refused to allow the liberating and empowering message of Christianity to be preached to them. Even today, the minorities who are also indigenes are denied access to land to build religious places of worship or schools that do not promote the major religion (Kukah 2018). Moreover, the Catholic Poverty Reduction Project had its house destroyed and a stern warning was sent to the organization not to attempt to reconstruct the building. Akinwale (2016) wrote:

> To be a Christian in Sokoto Diocese is to face the challenge of witnessing. … There is the insecurity of Churches and of those who worship in them. By now one would have lost count of how many times the Church and the Rectory in the town of Funtua have been burnt. On December 31, 1988, the Church of St Jude in Chafe was burnt. It has been rebuilt and burnt on at least one other occasion. … I recall the demolition of the Church in Isa. The location of the Cathedral of the Holy Family, hidden behind buildings, gives the impression that the Church in Sokoto is a Church in the catacombs. For decades, the city of Sokoto was a city with only one Catholic Church.

There is also the issue of forced marriage and conversion, especially in the core northern part of the country under the guise of religion (Elizabeth 2009). Most often these acts are perpetrated by highly placed politicians and religious leaders who hide under the garb of religion. For instance, *The Guardian* reported that "Senator Ahmed Sani Yerima, representative of Zamfara West in northern Nigeria, made headlines back in 2010 when he married a 13-year-old Egyptian girl. Three years later he persuaded his fellow senators to defeat a motion that would have removed a constitutional loophole according to which girls under age 18 are considered adults as soon as they get married" (Sandler Clarke 2015). Others have followed Yerima's lead, as shown in Table 2.

Even better known than these cases are the 276 missing Chibok girls kidnapped by Boko Haram in 2015 from their schools in Borno and Yobe states. In all these cases, the perpetrators of these acts were able to manipulate religious teaching in connivance with highly placed religious scholars and leaders.

These cases of forced underage marriage highlight a broader problem, as Nigeria has among the highest child marriage rates in the world. In Northern Nigeria, about 45% of girls are married – usually against their will – by age 15 and 73% by age 18. Adults who force such teenage girl brides into marriage hide under the guise of religion and tradition to carry out such practices, which are further fuelled by poverty, ignorance and illiteracy (Arukaino 2016). This contravenes the law of the land in light of the Child Rights Act of 2003, which raised the minimum age of marriage for girls to 18. But the legislation, which was created at the federal level, takes effect only if also approved by state governments. To date, only 24 of Nigeria's 36 states have passed the act (Sandler Clarke 2015).

8. The impact on northern minorities and national unity

It is clear that the basis for Nigeria's unity has been compromised and that the country, if the crisis is not well managed, could be heading for self-destruction. Most Nigerians are now apprehensive of the activities of Islamic fundamentalists

	Name of Victim	Age	Place	Case	Year
1	Lucy Ejeh	13	Zamfara	Forced marriage, conversion	2009
2	Patience Paul	Not stated	Abducted in Benue, married off in Sokoto	Forced marriage, conversion	2010
3	Marian Yerima (Egyptian)	13	Zamfara	Not stated	2010
4	Ifeoma Odugisi	14	Zaria	Forced marriage, conversion	2014
5	Blessing Gopep	13	Bauchi	Forced marriage, conversion	2015
6	Linda Christopher	16	Bauchi	Forced marriage, conversion	2015

Table 2: Cases of Forced Marriage, Conversion and Change of Name

and their constant threat to the corporate existence of the nation, and as such, a cross-section of Nigerians, especially from the southern part of the country as well as the northern minorities, are clamouring for the disintegration of the country. For example, in the religious realm, the Christian Association of Nigeria (the umbrella body for Christians in Nigeria) through its Secretary General has warned of retaliation that may lead to large-scale destruction and religious war, which Nigeria may not survive (Cocks and Onuah 2011).

Furthermore, ethnic militia groups have emerged in various parts of the country. For instance, in the north central area the Akhwat Akwop claims to represent the minor northern tribes and the Christian minority. Northern Christians and non-indigenes have disassociated themselves from this group, but in view of the high rate of reprisal killings in some parts of the country, especially the Jos area, one is forced to assume that the battle lines have already been drawn. In southwestern Nigeria, the O'odua Peoples Congress (OPC) asked all Yoruba indigenes to leave the north and return home. Similarly, the Igbo group Ogbunigwe Ndigbo also asked all Muslims (especially those of northern extraction) to leave the southeast part of Nigeria or face mass killings. Other militant groups include the Indigenous People of Biafra, the Movement for the Actualisation of the Sovereign State of Biafra and the Niger Delta Liberation Force.

Also, the National Youth Service Corps, which since the 1970s has acted as a catalyst for youth and national integration, has been greatly threatened by the activities of the dreaded Boko Haram sect, as corps members serving in most parts of northern Nigeria have been killed at random. As a result, youths from other parts of Nigeria have threatened to boycott national service henceforth.

9. Conclusion

From the foregoing, it is clear that Nigeria is facing serious security threats. The people of Nigeria, irrespective of their ethnic group, region or religion, should become much more alert and united and should work to expose and reject all forces aimed at destabilizing and destroying the nation's hard-earned democracy and its already fragile economy. Nigerians should be able to see through the activities and utterances of the fundamentalist groups and their related allies both within and outside the country, and they should be more active in promoting and defending inter-ethnic and inter-religious harmony within the country, as mutual co-operation has so much to offer to all of Nigeria's people.

Integration has progressed far enough in Nigeria that any attempt to legitimize the activities of the fundamentalists and their confused ideology would result in all of Nigeria sinking. The bitter experiences that the country has passed through and survived, from the struggle for independence through civil war and a period of military dictatorship, indicate that Nigerians can still stand together. However, this can be achieved only once we are able to set all religious sentiments aside and be honest and frank about the role of the fundamentalist sects and their destabilization of Nigeria.

References

Afigbo, A. E. 1981. "The Beni Mirage" and the history of south central Nigeria. *Nigeria Magazine*. Vol. 137, Federal Ministry of Sports and Culture, Lagos: 17-24.

Akinwale, A. 2016. Are there Christians in Sokoto? A history of Catholicism in the Caliphate. Paper presented at the Synod of the Diocese of Sokoto, 21–24 September 2016.

Akubor, E. O. 2011. Civil unrest in northern Nigeria: Beyond the literal "Boko Haram." *The Constitution: A Journal of Constitutional Development*, Centre for Constitutionalism and Demilitarisation (CENCOD), Lagos. 11, no. 4 (December): 71–93.

Akubor, E. O., and Akinwale, A. 2014. Sowing in the desert: Birth and growth of the Catholic Diocese of Sokoto. Nigeria: Catholic Diocese of Sokoto.

Akubor, E. O., and Musa, Gerald. 2018. The Maguzawa and Nigerian citizenship: Reflecting on identity politics and the national question in Africa. *Ufahamu: A Journal of African Studies* 41(1): 65–80.

Anfani, M. J. 2001. Split the core North. *Post Express*, 4 May.

Arukaino, U. 2016. Stolen child brides: Nigeria's hidden, ignored epidemic. *Punch*, 13 March.

Clark, S. 2004. Early marriage and HIV risks in sub-Saharan Africa. *Studies in Family Planning* 35(3): 149–58.

Cocks, T., and Onuah, F. 2011. Northern Nigerian Christians warn of religious war. Reuters, 27 December 2011.

Destexhe, Alan. 1995. *Rwanda and genocide in the twentieth century*. London: Pluto Press.

Ibe, Cyril. 1998. *Church and humanization, a viable possibility: The case of the Maguzawa of Nigeria*. Sokoto, Nigeria: Catholic Bishops' House.

Institute of Pastoral Affairs. 1989. Trends in Nigerian Christian-Muslim relations. Seminar on Contemporary Islam and Nigeria, Jos, Nigeria, 13–15 November.

Kukah, M. H. 2007. *The church and the politics of social responsibility*. Kaduna: Sovereign Print.

Kukah, M. H. 2018. Threats to the Christian faith in contemporary Nigeria. Keynote address at a conference of the Catholic Men's Guild, Archdiocese of Lagos, 16 June.

Kumolu, Charles. 2011. How Maitatsine raised curtain for militancy. *Vanguard*, 17 June.

Maier, K. 2000. *This house has fallen: Nigeria in crisis*. London: Penguin.

Onwudiwe, O, 2011. The North and the continued existence of Nigeria: The politics of change and revolution. *African Herald Express*, 18 July.

Paden, J. 1986. *Ahmadu Bello Sardauna of Sokoto: Values and leadership in Nigeria*. Zaria, Nigeria: Hudahuda Publishing Company.

Parrinder, G. 1969. *Africa's three religions*. London: Sheldon Press.

Prunier, Gerard. 1995. *The Rwanda crisis: history of a genocide*. London: Hurst & Company.

Sandler Clarke, J. 2015. Nigeria: Child brides facing death sentences a decade after child marriage prohibited. *The Guardian*, 11 March, https://www.theguardian.com/global-development-professionals-network/2015/mar/11/the-tragedy-of-nigerias-child-brides.

Smith, A. 1987. The early states of the Central Sudan, in *A little new light: Selected writings of Abdullahi Smith*, edited by G. Kwanashie et al. Zaria, Nigeria: Abdullahi Smith Centre for Historical Research.

Stewart, Scott. 2012. Nigeria's Boko Haram militants remain a regional threat. *The Nation*, 30 January.

US Bureau of Democracy, Human Rights, and Labor. 2010. Restrictions on religious freedom, Shari'a: Christians suffer religious persecution in Northern Nigeria.

Usman, Y. B. 1979. *For the liberation of Nigeria: Essays and lectures 1969–1978*. London: Beacon.

Yahaya, A. 2007. Socio-political conflicts in the Central Nigerian Area: A historical inquiry into the metropolitan Sharia conflict, in *Historical perspectives on Nigeria's postcolonial conflicts*, edited by Olayemi Akinwumi, Satu Fwatshak and Okpeh Okpeh. Lagos: Historical Society of Nigeria.

Yakub, I. 1992. The Maitatsine saga. *The Bloom*, 5(1), February.

Building our houses on sand
Exegetical implications of the Sermon on the Mount for religious freedom

Nicholas Kerton-Johnson[1]

Abstract

This article asks that we consider a vital question with regard to religious freedom: Does our response to hostility reflect Jesus' model and his call to expand the Kingdom of God? At the heart of the Christian defense of religious freedom is the call to be able to live according to the dictates of scripture, yet this places a burden on Christians to carefully consider whether we are, in fact, being obedient to the scriptures we seek to live by. This paper examines the Sermon on the Mount to reflect on the implications of Jesus' famous sermon for how we respond to religious freedom challenges and concludes that the primary defense of religious freedom is to be found in a church that actively lives out Jesus' Kingdom-advancing instructions.

Keywords: United States of America, religious freedom, responses, Christian ethics.

1. Introduction

Whatever the defining issues in any generation, there is no more authoritative definition of the Christian faith, Christian thinking and the Christian way of life than the supreme standard of Jesus himself, the good news of the kingdom of God that he announced, taught, demonstrated and advanced, including the supreme authority of scriptures that he endorsed and the power of the Spirit whom he sent.[2]

Central to the Christian defense of religious freedom is the desire to live in obedience to Scripture. However, if we are to make this demand, then we must in turn be faithful to the demands that Scripture makes of us. This paper explores our response to challenges to religious freedom, reflecting on the Kingdom of God and on Jesus' Sermon on the Mount as a foundationally important passage, which Jesus warned us to follow lest we build our house (our church and our freedom in this case) on sand.

---

[1] Dr. Nicholas Kerton-Johnson is an Associate Professor of International Relations and holds the R. Philip Loy Endowed Chair of Political Science at Taylor University. He is also lead pastor of Kingdom Life Church, Indiana, USA. This paper was first presented at the Henry Symposium for Religion and Public Life, Calvin College, Grand Rapids, Michigan, 30 April 2015. The paper uses American English. Article received: 24 August 2015; accepted: 28 January 2020. The author can be contacted at nckertonjohnson@taylor.edu.
[2] Os Guinness, *Renaissance: The Power of the Gospel However Dark the Times* (Downers Grove, IL: InterVarsity Press, 2014), 153.

It is common, in analyses of religious freedom, to concentrate on governmental and societal restrictions of religious freedom.[3] We often then interrogate these restrictions from an accepted vantage point – the Universal Declaration of Human Rights, US Bill of Rights or European Convention of Human Rights. However, we too seldom ask how communities of the faithful are responding to religious freedom challenges.[4]

In the US, law overwhelmingly dominates the religious freedom discussion, and this focus requires legal and not theological analysis.[5] Studies of the persecuted church such as Ronald Boyd-MacMillan's *Faith That Endures* and Glenn Penner's *In the Shadow of the Cross* do examine theological aspects of persecution, detailing the scriptural basis of a range of choices for Christians who face persecution.[6] Yet in the US, little attention is given to the nature of the Christian response.

In a democracy such as the US, it is appropriate for religious freedom to be contested in the courts and for vigorous political debates to lead to contestable legislation. Christians must inhabit the political world and advocate for religious freedom. As such, this paper is not a call for detachment from the world, but it rather seeks to reorient our focus, asking whether the church's current responses to religious freedom challenges are misguided or even harmful to the church. It is vital that Christians reflect very carefully on the strategies being employed, for it is likely that current approaches, especially in our media-saturated world, will not promote religious freedom but will rather heighten a distrust of the church and further empower its social marginalization. I believe that the most important question that should be animating our discussions of religious freedom within the church

---

[3] The Pew Research Center's work is preeminent in this regard. See for example "Rising Tide of Restrictions on Religion," http://www.pewforum.org/2012/09/20/rising-tide-of-restrictions-on-religion-findings/.

[4] The research project "Under Caesar's Sword: Christian Response to Persecution" being undertaken by the Center for Civil and Human Rights at Notre Dame is a leading example of efforts to pose such questions. Yet this project is an empirical analysis, rather than a critique of Christian responses to suffering. The latter deserves greater attention.

[5] The research which inspired this article is focused on the US, and is hence written with a US focus. However, I would hope that the biblical lessons discussed here would be applicable to Christians across the world. Much of what I write reflects the witness that I have observed from many Christians in countries where extreme persecution exists.

[6] Ronald Boyd-MacMillan, *Faith That Endures* (Grand Rapids: Fleming H. Revell, 2006); Glenn Penner, *In the Shadow of the Cross: A Biblical Theology of Persecution and Discipleship* (Bartlesville, OK: Living Sacrifice Books, 2004). Penner summarizes the Christian choices as resisting, fleeing, avoiding and enduring. Penner contends that enduring is the most common biblical and historical pattern, followed by fleeing. Many Christians who advance a legal defense argument correctly cite Paul as a key example of using legal rights (his Roman citizenship) to defend against mistreatment. It is highly ironic, however, that they fail to recognize that Paul's actions were all for the purpose of fulfilling his mission – even unto death, a death that he anticipated following a prophetic encounter (Acts 21:10–13). Using legal defense to pursue a path to persecution hardly seems persuasive!

in the United States goes largely unasked. That question is as follows: Does our response to hostility reflect Jesus' model and his call to expand the Kingdom of God?[7]

2. Kingdom and Culture

As Christians, we must understand clearly that our primary value is not freedom to express our faith but rather opportunities to expand the Kingdom of God, for this is ultimately what Jesus' example calls us to do. Studies analyzing the political consequences of religious freedom responses are valuable, but their focus is on earthly models and outcomes. Jesus calls us to a prior commitment, and we must assess our actions against His words and model. We must engage with religious freedom issues in a manner that moves the church from political and cultural warrior, or the rather ridiculous status of 'defender of God', to being the active agent of God's Kingdom on earth – selflessly serving the world while at the same time knowing that this very selfless living will most powerfully attain the freedom which we crave. In short, the church, not the courts, must become the primary protector of religious freedom.

As Steve Garber has argued, culture is upstream from politics.[8] The political realm is just one realm in our society, and in the case of religious freedom it has been too readily separated from the wider Christian witness. Although contesting political authority and judicial rulings is necessary in our democracy, we are wrong if we consider this our primary focus. Not only does this method misread cultural change, but it is not loyal to the gospel. Engaging in culture provides many possibilities, as Andy Crouch and James Davison Hunter have shown.[9] However, Christian cultural engagement has too often been characterized as warfare, and Christians have too readily embraced the fear-based, loud and antagonistic strategies of the world. We have not sought to use language that the world can understand (to borrow from Steve Garber), nor have we borne witness to the Kingdom that we represent.

I am concerned that the American church has too readily adapted Pilate's paradigm of power in its political engagement with American culture. Engagement in politics itself is not the issue. Rather, the question is the type of power we are trying to exercise and the goals we are trying to achieve. The maintenance of a "Christian nation" status quo has largely dictated the American church's political approach for

---

[7] Of course, many important ideas can also be drawn from the New Testament, particularly from Acts and Paul's epistles. However, covering all these passages would require a book-length treatment of the subject. This paper holds that the gospels are paramount and that the Sermon on the Mount is central to our understanding of Christian engagement in society.

[8] Steven Garber, "The Culture Is Upstream from Politics", Washington Institute for Faith, Vocation and Culture, https://washingtoninst.org/the-culture-is-upstream-from-politics/.

[9] Andy Crouch, *Culture Making: Recovering Our Creative Calling* (Downers Grove, IL: InterVarsity Press, 2008); James Davison Hunter, *To Change the World: The Irony, Tragedy, and Possibility of Christianity in the Late Modern World* (New York: Oxford University Press, 2010).

the past few decades and embodies a triumphalism, an arrogant or self-righteous confidence that does not reflect the Kingdom of Jesus. It is time to question whether such an approach is nothing more than a power play that seeks control over the cultural environment by legislating against trends in the culture that make it a more uncomfortable place for the church to exist. In short, the political approach and paradigm of the religious right could easily be compared to the paradigm in which Pilate operated two thousand years ago. Most importantly, this approach is only increasing the animosity between the church and the wider culture and driving ever more forcefully the growing hatred towards the church.

We are, as Os Guinness warns, captive of the very modernity that our faith helped produce, imprisoned by comfort and a view of reality that is more secular than supernatural.[10] Christianity is a documented culture changer, but as Paul reminded the Corinthians (1 Cor 4:20), the gospel is not just one of words but of power. But this is not worldly power. This is a Spirit-infused power that enabled transformation through the lives of a handful of faithful men and women. To quote Guinness again: "But that transforming power is precisely what must be understood all over again, re-experienced and demonstrated once more in our time."[11] We in the church err when we leave such transformation to lawyers and politicians who fight downstream from cultural change, and we are wrong when we utilize only the methods of the world – advertising, social media and other formulas – to transform culture. The power of the gospel lies not just in believing it to be true but in living according to its radical nature.

John Stott argued that for the evangelical, Jesus is our model. His actions and words stand as the most imperative guide for our choices.[12] N. T. Wright goes further, arguing not only that Jesus is our model, but that the Church has too often covered up the calling to bring the Kingdom of God. Wright emphasizes that we are called to follow the Jesus of Scripture and not one of our own making.[13]

There are of course many different interpretations of what this Kingdom encompasses, but we principally make use of George Elton Ladd's characterization, defined as follows: "When the word refers to God's Kingdom, it always refers to His reign, His rule, His sovereignty, and not to the realm in which it is exercised."[14]

---

[10] Guinness, *Renaissance*, 37.

[11] Guinness, *Renaissance*, 21.

[12] John Stott, *Christ in Conflict: Lessons from Jesus and His Controversies* (Downers Grove, IL: InterVarsity Press, 2013).

[13] N. T. Wright, *The Challenge of Jesus: Rediscovering Who Jesus Was and Is* (Downers Grove, IL: InterVarsity Press, 1999), 7, 17, 93.

[14] George Eldon Ladd, *Gospel of the Kingdom: Scriptural Studies in the Kingdom of God* (Grand Rapids: Eerdmans, 1959), 20.

Jesus' Kingdom is not of this world, and it reigns when its revealing defeats the kingdom of this age.

"There is a very real and a very vital sense in which God has already manifested His reign, His will, His Kingdom, in the coming of Christ in the flesh, by virtue of which we may experience the life of the Kingdom here and now."[15] The gospel offers us the great promise that we need not live any longer according to the flesh or the world's standards. The power of the Kingdom of God – His rule – enables Kingdom living.

The Sermon on the Mount is a powerful exemplar of a Kingdom-oriented life, and in this discourse, perhaps Jesus' most famous one, we find a serious challenge to honestly judge our actions. Jesus says in Matthew 7:24–26 (NKJV):

> Therefore whoever hears these sayings of Mine, and does them, I will liken him to a wise man who built his house on the rock: and the rain descended, the floods came, and the winds blew and beat on that house; and it did not fall, for it was founded on the rock. But everyone who hears these sayings of Mine, and does not do them, will be like a foolish man who built his house on the sand: and the rain descended, the floods came, and the winds blew and beat on that house; and it fell. And great was its fall.

These words should encourage deep reflection because they speak prophetically to the current condition in which we find ourselves. If we utilize the tactics of the world, we will fail. If we utilize political tactics that do not reflect the gospel of Christ, we will fail. Even if such tactics appear to succeed, we will create a church that is a poor imitation of what Christ called us to, a church that God may well choose to dismantle Himself! If we are to be likened to men who build a house that can withstand rain, floods and high winds, we must give careful attention to Jesus' words. We are concerned that some of our methods in responding are effectively building our houses on sand, and it may well be that some of the challenges facing the church today are there precisely because we have forgotten to live as Christ lived and are reaping the rewards of our complacency towards His Kingdom.

3. Research Motivation

The foundation for this analysis of responses to perceived incursions on religious freedom has evolved from research carried out in Taylor University's political science department. In 2014 we tracked over 300 instances of some form of aggression against Christians in the United States.[16] Wherever possible, we investigated

---

[15] Ladd, *Gospel of the Kingdom*, 24.

[16] Steven Paku, Aaron Johnson, Abby Brockelsby, Suzanne Neefus, Carolina Alvarado, Chip Mironas, David Chiu, Kayla Gotha and Brian Charbogian assisted in the accumulation of this data.

the response by victims to the opposition they experienced. We categorized these responses according to a range of methods used by Christians to respond to threats, including acceptance, protests, adaptation, missional engagement, and legal action. We then classified the responses of Christians by how they seemed to positively or negatively represent the kingdom and mission of Christ, ranging from missional responses that sought to engage oppressors with love and redemption (which we deemed most positive) to combative, antagonistic, or hateful behavior that caused tangible harm to the witness of Christ.

We found in our cases that the predominant response (71%) was legal action. Legal action is in many cases neutral, a democratic act and a method of protecting religious freedom that many millions of persecuted religious minorities yearn for. However, in examining the "Kingdom" nature of the responses more broadly we found that fewer than 4% of responses could be characterized as very positive in their Kingdom building, where victims engaged the opposition with love and grace. A further 14% were classified as moderately positive. Fifteen percent of cases were damaging to Kingdom building in the sense that the action taken perpetuated culture war, division, and animosity without making an effort toward reconciliation. Our analysis indicates a deficit in creative thinking about how the church could positively respond to opposition in a way that pursues rather than alienates the culture.

4. The Sermon on the Mount

In Matthew 5–7, Jesus describes ways of living, being and worship that represent the Kingdom of God. These chapters give clear clues as to what God's kingdom encompasses, and most of the messages do not sit easily with our Western mindset and lifestyles. The Kingdom of God runs like a fine fragrance throughout these verses. Familiarity with these verses can cause us to miss their truth, and in missing their truth we not only miss their power but position our works outside the Kingdom – essentially, as Jesus warns, on sand.

As Christians, we must be willing to question our assumptions and traditions to ensure we do not stray from the biblical witness. After all, as Stott forcefully argues, "What is required is that we obey the Bible. The best way to honor this book as God's book is to do what it says."[17] The church is duty-bound to hold to the truth as revealed in the Bible, and Christians are thus "conservative" in Stott's description. However, the Christian is also duty-bound to be as radical as Scripture commands and is free to be as radical as the Bible allows.[18] As Christians engage with hostility

---

[17] Stott, *Christ in Conflict*, 96.
[18] Stott, *Christ in Conflict*, 33.

against their faith, they too often reflect the anti-Roman revolutionaries or isolated religious groups to whom Jesus offered an alternate vision of the Kingdom.[19] Rather, Matthew 5–7 includes a litany of descriptions of Kingdom-style living, most of which should give us profound reason for introspection.

Matthew 5 begins with the Beatitudes, where Jesus declares that the blessing of heaven would flow to those who hungered for righteousness, who were merciful, who were pure in heart and worked for peace. Those who seek peace are called "sons of God" (5:9). As for those who are persecuted for righteousness' sake, theirs is the kingdom of heaven. These verses offer us great encouragement to remain faithful to Christ and to His righteousness. They seem counter-intuitive, but verse 12 gives the first hint that something otherworldly is truly occurring here, for Jesus says to those who are persecuted, "Rejoice and be exceedingly glad, for great is your reward in heaven." This is a superhuman reaction, made possible only by the presence of the Spirit who becomes the source of this unnatural joy.

In verse 13, Jesus tells His followers that they are salt and light. Salt purifies and light shines in the darkness. These verses are often referenced by Christians who see themselves as standing apart from the ways of the world yet seeking to bring Jesus into the world's brokenness. But this section ends with the words, "Let your light so shine before men that they may see your *good works* (emphasis added) and glorify your Father in heaven." Salt and light are not just a matter of being but of doing, and our actions as salt and light are to be of such character that "men," not just believers, will glorify God. Salt by its very nature penetrates food to the point that it dissolves. So too are we to influence the world with our presence infused in society. This is not exemplified in legal action but in the sacrificial kingdom living that Jesus preached.

We are then challenged that "unless your righteousness exceeds the righteousness of the Pharisees, you will by no means enter the kingdom of heaven." This righteousness is assured to us through Jesus' death – it is His righteousness that we receive. Yet in the following verses He describes the nature of a righteous heart, of those who represent His kingdom. Murder is no longer a physical act alone; rather, the very speaking of the word "fool" places the speaker "in danger of hell fire." Similarly, the standard for adultery is remarkably adjusted; it is no longer the sexual act alone but lustful looks that reveal an unrighteous heart at risk of being "cast into hell."

Clearly the Kingdom's standards are different from those of the world. But Jesus is far from finished, and even as these statements must have shocked His audience, we must allow their truth to challenge us. We must be wary that our responses to

---

[19] Wright, *The Challenge of Jesus*, 37.

hostility do not include hate, name-calling and denigration of those who oppose us, for in doing so we will clearly step outside the values of His kingdom.

Perhaps most important for our purpose of interrogating religious freedom responses, verses 38–42 deal with turning the other cheek when struck and going beyond the onerous demands of those who mete out injustice: "If anyone wants to sue you and take away your tunic, let him have your cloak also. And whoever compels you to go one mile, go with him two" (5:40–41). How do we interpret this Scripture when we consider a homosexual couple suing a Christian baker for refusing to bake a cake? Should the Christian bake two cakes, or perhaps cut the price in half? While I am supportive of the position of non-service (and still believe that an ideal pluralistic society should allow such a choice), are we willing to consider whether, from Christ's perceptive, this constitutes walking the extra mile? Can a Christian make clear his or her objection and then say, "I will bake two cakes and not just one"?[20] Are we tainted by the sin of such actions, or could acts done in obedience to Jesus' command bring the Kingdom of God? As in much of the Sermon on the Mount, Jesus' approach is counter-intuitive, but this is the point: can we appreciate that the ways of the Kingdom may vary from our traditions? Jesus is asking his followers to go beyond even what those who persecute us demand. To emphasize this still further, in Matthew 5:43–44, Jesus speaks to the heart of his Kingdom in its most explicit character:

> But I say to you, love your enemies, bless those who curse you, do good to those who hate you, and pray for those who spitefully use you and persecute you, that you may be *sons of your Father in heaven* (emphasis added).

Is there anything more counter-cultural to us? Is there anything more revealing about the state of our own hearts and our tendency to rely on worldly, power-based responses when we are the subjects and victims of hatred? Do we love? As Ladd argues:

> The righteousness of the Kingdom of God demands an attitude of heart which is not motivated by selfish concerns, which does not demand evening one's wrong and which is free from the motivation of personal vindication.[21]

Who in the United States is the Samaritan, the outsider, the person with whom you should not associate? Who is the prostitute, the sick, who needs the Doctor's pres-

---

[20] Cases involving provision of service are increasing in the US. These are complex issues, but Jesus' command in Matthew 5:41 does at the very least demand that we carefully consider our responses.

[21] Ladd, *Gospel of the Kingdom*, 89.

ence (Mark 2:17)? Do we see that to be sons of God is to be those who love? We have become so accustomed to speaking the truth that we have forgotten that truth must be administered within the bounds of love. The greatest danger that we face in adopting the world's strategies is that Kingdom-defined love cannot be present.

There are other challenges in these chapters, perhaps not as relevant to religious freedom issues, but which speak to the nature of our hearts and the extent to which they mirror God's Kingdom. We are told to let our charitable deeds be done in secret (6:1–4) so as to please God, and not seek the praise of man. We are taught to pray in private, not seeking the praise of man for our religious efforts (6:5–6). Fasting is to be done in secret, and we are told not to store earthly treasures (6:16–21). All these messages seek to cultivate a people whose hearts seek the well-being of others above their own reputation.

Chapter 7 begins with Jesus calling us not to judge. This is not to say that we cannot speak out against unrighteousness, but that a spirit of arrogance that ignores our own shortcomings is hypocritical. We must therefore ask ourselves whether our hearts and mouths are governed by humility and whether we rank sins, tolerating some and not others.

Perhaps the most troubling verses are 7:21–23. Here Jesus refuses entry into His kingdom to many people. What should especially worry us is that this group of people appears to be manifesting great power in their lives – casting out demons and healing the sick, all in Jesus' name. Yet Jesus' primary desire is for us to know Him. If we are to know Him, we must be in relationship with Him and obedient to Him, not to legalism. In John 14:21, Jesus makes clear that only those who keep His commands truly love Him and will in turn be loved and will experience His presence.

Finally, Jesus presents His analogy of a house built on sand. This is a statement of profound importance. If our works are not in alignment with Christ's commands, then we will be building our house, our defense and our churches on sand. It is not enough to be righteous in our application of biblical truth to social issues, seeking political solutions and ultimately political control. This is not the victory of God's rule, as if political victory will necessarily represent His will. We must love our enemies, and the witness of this love attests to the watching world that we are of Christ. Our failure to live the radical, spirit-infused life weakens the gospel, making us less credible at best, hypocrites at worst. As Guinness argues, the "American way of life has moved far from the life of Jesus – which means simply that the Christians who are the majority are living a way of life closer to the world than to the way of Jesus. In a word, they are worldly and therefore incapable of shaping their culture."[22] We must recognize that the practice of Christian truth carries enormous power: "When

---

[22] Guinness, *Renaissance*, 60.

followers of Jesus live out the gospel in the world, as we are called to do, we become an incarnation of the truth of the gospel, and an expression of the character
and shape of its truth. It is this living-in-truth that proves culturally powerful."[23]

To be clear, the nature of the life that Jesus commands is not within human
capabilities. As Ladd argues, "The righteousness of the Kingdom is a righteousness
which only God can give. The righteousness which God's Kingdom demands, God's
Kingdom must give. ... I can manifest the life of the Kingdom only as I have experienced it."[24] We forgive because we are forgiven. We have compassion because
He has shown us mercy. As the parable of the indebted servant shows, our Father
expects us to forgive those who owe far less than we owed Him. Too often, even
within our churches, we fail to reflect this reality of the Kingdom – let alone in our
relationships with those who oppose us. As Ladd argues, "Kingdom righteousness
demands that I have no evil in my heart towards my fellow man. It is obvious that
such a heart righteousness can itself be only the gift of God. God must give what He
demands."[25]

We must begin to honestly appraise our interaction with the broken world
around us and ask whether we are falling short of the commands of our Savior. For
if we are falling short, we are building on sand and our work will collapse. Frankly,
we should expect nothing else, for we are very likely building our own kingdom
and not His.

5. Conclusion

The 16th-century scholar Thomas Linacre reacted to his first reading of the gospels
by saying, "Either these are not the gospels, or we are not Christians!"[26] Even as
we confront challenges to religious freedom from the culture around us, we must
be aware that a loss of spiritual awareness and of a vital commitment to Scripture
brings a cultural secularization within the church, something far more dangerous to our witness than any imposition by the state.[27] Are we similarly liable to
Kierkegaard's accusation that "The Christianity of the New Testament simply does
not exist"?[28] As evangelicals, we may be quick to point such fingers to liberalizing
wings of the Church as it supports unbiblical positions on Jesus' divinity or sexual

---

[23] Guinness, *Renaissance*, 75.
[24] Ladd, *Gospel of the Kingdom*, 93.
[25] Ladd, *Gospel of the Kingdom*, 83.
[26] Os Guinness, "Found Faithful: Standing Fast in Faith in the Advanced Modern Era," in Richard Lints, *Renewing the Evangelical Mission* (Grand Rapids: Eerdmans, 2013), 105.
[27] Guinness, *Renaissance*, 115.
[28] Søren Kierkegaard, *Attack upon "Christendom"*, trans. Walter Lowrie (Princeton: Princeton University Press, 1968), 32-33.

sin, yet have we also lost hold of the more difficult demands that Jesus makes on our lives? Have we chosen in our own way that which is more comfortable or palatable?

Wright argues, "The way of Christian witness is neither the way of quietest withdrawal, nor the way of Herodian compromise, nor the way of angry militant zeal. It is the way of being in Christ, in the Spirit, at the place where the world is in pain, so that the healing love of God may be brought to bear at this point."[29] It might be that our greatest challenge is not new restrictions on religious freedom by a culture that is shifting so dramatically from Christian orthodoxy, but rather that God is calling for a people who will live according to the radical nature of the Scriptures they purport to love and seek to defend their right to follow. For only in living by the Spirit of God, being Jesus' ambassadors in the world, can have any true hope of transforming the culture around us. Like the early church, we are ambassadors of a new world order.[30]

As the Church, we are called to be in but not of the world. Clearly, there are times when we must not conform or comply with anything that is contrary to the way of Jesus and the Kingdom He preached. Yet in not conforming to the world, we too often fail to represent the heart of God to the broken world around us.[31]. The Holy Spirit will give us a curious distaste for the things of the world but a deep love for its people. Indeed, the Kingdom is characterized by our ability to love those who hate us the most. As Guinness argues, "What changes the world is not a fully developed Christian worldview, but a worldview actually lived – in other words, in Christian lives that are the Word made flesh."[32] If we live otherwise, our efforts will be rooted in our human gifts and not in the spiritual-human partnership that Jesus inaugurated.

Our failure to reflect on the Kingdom of God and walk according to its tenets is not neutral but destructive. As Ladd emphatically argues:

> The primary manifestation of satanic influence and of the evil of This Age is religious; it is the blindness with reference to the Gospel of Jesus Christ. How often we fail to understand satanic devices! A man may be a cultured, ethical and even religious person and yet be in demonic darkness. Satan's basic desire is to keep men from Christ. His primary concern is not to corrupt morals nor make atheists nor to produce enemies of religions. Indeed, religion which rests upon the assumption

---

[29] Wright, *The Challenge of Jesus*, 189.

[30] Wright, *The Challenge of Jesus*, 164.

[31] Guinness, *Renaissance*, 84.

[32] Guinness, *Renaissance*, 86; see also Wright, *The Challenge of Jesus*, 184–187.

of human adequacy and sufficiency is an enemy of the light. This is the character of the Age of this world: darkness.[33]

Jesus did not come to build a religion. He came to bring a Kingdom – the kingdom of God's rule and reign – but it is by the Spirit that this is achieved. Jesus' Kingdom was not of this world, and as such it did not follow the world's methods, empowered by the sword. His Kingdom was empowered by the Spirit. We too quickly shift our focus away from this reality to the methodology of our age rather than trusting that the power that birthed the Christian church is still available to followers of Christ today. Are we trusting God and willing to live lives faithful to the gospel, articulating a "vision of the kingdom of God" that can carry us through this time of turmoil?[34]

Religious freedom in the US is dominated by legal defense. Not only does this emphasis distort the Christian witness to the society around us, but it causes Christians to delegate their ambassadorial role to a few. Every Christian is called to represent the Kingdom of God in their spheres of influence – family, friends, corporate life, church and wider world. Rank-and-file Christians should be encouraged to see that their lives, their choices, and their willingness to live by the gospel of Jesus are powerful agents for the protection of religious freedom. The Church must be taught that it is the primary defense of religious freedom – not by public protests or by funding legal groups (although both may be necessary at times) but through imitating the biblical record of Christian triumph that reveals victory through sacrificial love and a Kingdom-oriented lifestyle. In this defense of religious freedom, every Christian plays a role.

Christian leaders and scholars must continue to articulate a vision of Kingdom expansion that is built on the counter-cultural and supernatural approach of Jesus. History records the incredibly positive and indeed foundational role that the church has played in the formation of our society. We should, like Jesus, be able to ask those who oppose our faith, "Many good works I have shown you from My Father. For which of those works do you stone me?" (John 10:32).

---

[33] Ladd, *Gospel of the Kingdom,* 31.
[34] Guinness, *Renaissance,* 23.

Problems that result from granting freedom of religious exercise to US corporations

Thomas E. Simmons[1]

Abstract

The U.S. Supreme Court's 2014 *Hobby Lobby* decision was widely heralded as a victory for proponents of religious freedom. In *Hobby Lobby*, a closely held corporation was permitted to claim the right of religious exercise and thereby avoid a government mandate that infringed upon the shareholders' religious beliefs. But the rationale underpinning that decision is problematic, because it invoked the entity theory of corporate personhood. That rationale contains pitfalls for any religious rights held by faith entities. Specifically, the tax-exempt status of faith-entities could be made more vulnerable by the endorsement of entity theory in the context of religious freedom issues.

Keywords   Religious corporations, closely held corporations, tax-exempt entities, nonprofits, Hobby Lobby, aggregate theory, entity theory.

In the realm of law, a "person" may be either a human being or an artificial person, such as a corporation. This paper explores whether religious artificial persons (such as churches, temples, mosques, or even for-profit enterprises) should enjoy religious freedom rights separate from the individual members of those entities. I analyze the question from the perspective of United States jurisprudence, beginning with the *Hobby Lobby* decision, which recognized the ability of closely held corporations to hold religious freedom rights independently of their shareholders.[2] I then compare the decision to two primary corporate theories – aggregate theory and entity theory – and conclude that *Hobby Lobby*'s implicit application of the entity theory to corporate personhood in the context of religious freedom may be problematic. Although the cause of religious freedom prevailed in *Hobby Lobby*, the underlying rationale is troublesome. Specifically, an instinctive or automatic application of entity theory with regard to religious matters could jeopardize the tax-exempt status of a nonprofit entity. Moreover, entity theory misconstrues the reality of most collective religious observances.

1. An introduction to entity and aggregate theories

There are many varieties of artificial legal persons, such as corporations, partnerships, and estates. Much of business organizations law in the 20th century ques-

---

[1]   Thomas E. Simmons is a professor at the University of South Dakota School of Law in Vermillion, South Dakota, USA, where he has taught Business Organizations I and II. Email: tom.e.simmons@usd.edu. This paper uses American spelling. Article received: 1 November 2016; accepted: 6 December 2019.
[2]   *Burwell v. Hobby Lobby Stores*, Inc., 573 U.S. 682, 134 S.Ct. 2751 (2014) (hereinafter *Hobby Lobby*).

tioned whether one of the prime structures for small businesses – the partnership – was merely a collection of partners or an independent actor in its own right. Aggregate theory presumes that although an entity shell can be recognized to some degree, the partnership, at its core, is simply an assemblage of natural persons (i.e., human beings) who have gathered together to pursue a shared aim. In contrast, entity theory, while acknowledging the interests of the various human constituents, understands the partnership itself as an entity and thus acknowledges the partnership's independent existence as an artificial person to a greater degree than aggregate theory.

Entity theory and aggregate theory might be viewed more as points on a continuum than as in direct opposition to each other.[3] Entity theory is biased toward the personhood of the partnership and views partnerships as organizations. Aggregate theory favors the constituents of the partnership; it considers partnerships as "constitutive communities which are constructed out of normatively thick collective affiliations in which individual members regard their own good as intimately connected to the good of the group."[4] The basic doctrinal issue in the early part of the 20th century was which theory, aggregate or entity, best captured the 'true' nature of a partnership.

This question had no easy solution, since it was embedded in the theoretical and rather abstract structure of artificial persons. An artificial legal person could be at once a subject (a unit bearing rights) and an object (alienable and malleable). With regard to corporate subjects, identifying any particular event as representative of 'corporate will' was an unclear matter, which was initially resolved by requiring shareholder unanimity, at least on fundamental issues. "Unanimous consent for fundamental changes was needed, in part, because the corporation formed a contractual triad between the parties which could not be altered but for the consent of all."[5] After all, if a mere majority could represent the will of the corporate entity – and bind the dissenting minority – "the 'corporate will' had to mean something other than the actual consent of the entity."[6] But soon, it came to mean just that. A rather uniquely American innovation, born out of the demands of commercial enterprise, claimed that a corporation could be an independent legal person. "American law, unlike its British progenitor, began to view the corporation as a construct which could be divorced from both its human constituent parts and the economic reality in which it existed."[7] Partnerships would follow the same evolution in fits and starts.

---

[3] James D. Nelson, *Conscience, Incorporated,* Michigan State Law Review 1565, 1583 (2013).

[4] *Id.*

[5] Brett W. King, "The Use of Supermajority Voting Rules in Corporate America: Majority Rule, Corporate Legitimacy, and Minority Shareholder Protection", 21 Del J. Corp. L. 895, 900 (1996).

[6] *Id.*

[7] Id. See also John Dewey, "The Historic Background of Corporate Legal Personality", 35 Yale L.J. 655,

In the United States, the 1914 Uniform Partnership Act (UPA), drafted by the National Conference of Commissioners on Uniform State Laws, gave a mixed answer to the question of aggregate or entity, suggesting that a partnership represented an independent legal person (an entity) but was also a collection of flesh-and-blood persons oriented toward a shared aim (an aggregate).[8] The UPA thus situated partnerships at a midpoint on the aggregate–entity continuum. It was an awkward compromise. Some speculated that the hybridization of aggregate and entity theories in the UPA could be traced to the untimely death of Dean Ames, a proponent of the entity theory and reporter for the drafting committee, about halfway through the project.[9] The same debate echoes in questions of religious freedoms when artificial legal persons are involved.

Application of the entity theory to worship-oriented organizations – churches, temples, mosques – as well as to religiously infused entities dominated by devout individuals (hereinafter, both types will be referenced collectively as "faith entities") – resulted in gains for proponents of religious freedom. An entity theory for faith entities seemingly amplifies religious liberty. It expands the number of potential persons (i.e., both natural persons and artificial persons) who can assert a religious right. The ability of an artificial legal person, whether nonprofit or for-profit, to claim religious rights for itself can achieve the extension of those rights to corporate actors and constituents in areas where persecution might otherwise go unchallenged. In this sense, applying entity theory to faith entities is a good thing. Conversely, the alternative theory, aggregate personhood, may cost the faithful some degree of religious freedom by depopulating the list of potential claimants who can assert religious rights.

However, entity theory, as the alternative to aggregate personhood, is not all good, nor does it necessarily rest on an accurate construction of religious practice. Entities can do certain things as persons (such as entering into contracts or committing wrongs), but they cannot do all the things that natural persons can. Entities cannot obtain a high-school diploma, for example. Most understandings of religious acts, from worship to prayer, would not support an entity's ability to practice religion. Nor do religious beliefs or matters of faith typically reside within a corporate actor. And when courts or legislators pretend otherwise, unintended consequences may result.

It should be acknowledged that some sorts of religious exercises *do* involve an entity and therefore fit to a greater degree with entity theory. Evangelization, mis-

---

667–678 (1926) (contrasting "fiction" and "concession" theories of corporate rights).

[8]   See the Uniform Partnership Act § 6(1) (1914).

[9]   See *id.*, Commissioners' Prefatory Note (narrating how Harvard Law School's Dean had been secured in 1903 as the drafting committee's reporter but that he had died in 1910, after which the "experts present recommended that the act be drawn on the aggregate or common law theory").

sionary work, and approving or rejecting official statements of dogma are carried out to a large degree by a faith entity acting as such. Thus, in these instances, an entity might be seen as the actor. To a lesser degree, the implementation and oversight of ceremonies or sacraments are more akin to conduct by an entity than are acts of worship or praise. However, these modest exceptions, in which a religious organization acts more like an entity than as an assemblage of individuals, reinforce the broader assertion that most religious exercises do not involve an entity-actor as such. When we permit the entity theory to be applied to the religious viewpoints of a corporation, the theory becomes "divorced from observable reality."[10] If worship and salvation form the nucleus of a religion, then the core of religious practice centers on the individual rather than the collective.

If an unacknowledged falsehood resides within the entity theory concerning the nature of most religious impulses, one might say that its application in this context is dishonest. Dishonesty has public-relations costs in terms of presenting an inaccurate picture of religion to nonbelievers. But it may have legal consequences as well. I propose one potential, undesirable consequence of an unthinking embrace of entity theory: it could give tax authorities a powerful tool by which to police worship that carries political overtones and thereby withdraw favorable exempt status with alarming frequency.

In the following discussion, I focus on the nature of mainstream Catholic and Protestant worship and how it is constructed within faith entities. Other religious traditions, including Islam, Judaism, and Buddhism as well as certain Christian traditions, may share some commonalities with mainstream Christian collective religious experiences, but they also differ in material respects. To that extent, my assertions should be read as giving way to various and disparate religious practices as required. Variations in religious tenets do not permit reflexive shoehorning of arguments. Religions differ and my arguments likely fit some religious practices more than others. It is not my intent to suggest otherwise nor to impose any sort of value judgment which favors some religions over others.

2. The *Hobby Lobby* case

One of the most important events in recent American religious-freedom jurisprudence is the Supreme Court's 2014 *Hobby Lobby* decision. This decision confronted – but did not analyze – the impact of entity and aggregate theories in the context of religious freedom.[11] Though widely celebrated for upholding religious liberties, the Supreme Court's ruling actually addressed religious freedom only obliquely while

---

[10] Matthew J. Allman, Note, "Swift Boat Captains of Industry for Truth: Citizens United and the Illogic of Natural Person Theory of Corporate Personhood", 38 Fla. St. U. L. Rev. 387, 388 (2011).

[11] *Hobby Lobby*, 573 U.S. 682, 134 S.Ct. 2751.

relying on an entity theory of corporate personhood. The narrow legal question before the Court was whether the U.S. Congress intended the word "person" in its Religious Freedom Restoration Act (RFRA) to include closely held corporations.[12]

Hobby Lobby has merited study for its impact on the free exercise of religion, but the Court merely decided, as a matter of statutory construction, that the word "person" in RFRA does refer to closely held corporations (artificial legal persons) as well as to individuals (natural persons). The Court did not consider whether corporations *ought* to enjoy religious rights. Prior law had already recognized nonprofit corporations as qualifying as persons under RFRA.[13] The Court reasoned that "no conceivable definition of the term includes natural persons and nonprofit corporations, but not for-profit corporations."[14] After all, for-profit corporations, though primarily oriented toward making money, often pursue altruistic objectives just as nonprofits (including churches) do. Some for-profit corporations, for example, make charitable donations to religious enterprises. Some may be dominated by officers and directors who are religiously minded. Some reject sinful business practices even if those practices are lawful and profitable.

Viewed with this gloss, *Hobby Lobby* is actually a relatively unimportant ruling; its holding is narrow and unlikely to impact future controversies under the common law doctrine of *stare decisis*. Justice Samuel Alito, writing for the majority of the Court, simply reasoned that it was inconsistent for the word "person" in a particular statutory context to encompass nonprofit corporations but not for-profit corporations. Both are artificial legal persons, both are convenient legal constructions, and neither is more like an actual flesh-and-blood person than the other. Both are legal fictions; neither is genuinely a person. Personhood for corporations generally, and for faith entities in particular, is and always has been simply a convenient construction, a product of commercial necessity.

In addition to the distinctions between for-profit faith entities and their nonprofit counterparts evinced above, the unique character of closely held or family-owned faith entities also deserves mention. Some sources of legal authority suggest that the mere number of shareholders is irrelevant to questions of personhood. One case proclaims, for example, "The fact that one person owns all of the stock does not make him and the corporation one and the same person."[15] The extension of religious rights to a corporation wholly owned by a single religious human being cannot necessarily be equated with the extension of religious rights to a publicly

---

[12] Religious Freedom Restoration Act of 1993, Pub. L. No. 103-141, 107 Stat. 1488 (Nov. 16, 1993), codified at 42 U.S.C. §§ 2000bb through 2000bb-4 (2016).

[13] See *Gonzales v. O Centro Espirita Beneficente Uniao do Vegetal,* 546 U.S. 418 (2006) (entertaining a RFRA claim brought by a nonprofit entity).

[14] *Hobby Lobby,* 134 S.Ct. at 2769.

[15] *Barium Steel Corp. v. Wiley,* 108 A.2d 336, 341 (Pa. 1954) (applying corporate veil piercing doctrine).

traded institution, however. Searching for the religious locus in a corporation with millions of ever-shifting shareholders is unlike the assessment one might undertake for a single-shareholder corporation.

As noted above, close-knit shareholders of a family enterprise often pursue goals other than the maximization of profits. For example, Hobby Lobby committed its family owners to "honoring the Lord in all [they] do by operating the company in a manner consistent with Biblical principles."[16] The presumed primary goal for large corporations with numerous unrelated shareholders, by contrast, is profitability. Closely held corporations are more frequently endowed with aims other than mere profit.

A second important distinction between closely held and larger corporations is the liquidity of larger entities' shares of stock (representing an easy exit strategy), which smaller organizations often lack. Shareholders of smaller organizations have a greater tendency to be stuck with their status in the enterprise. The *Hobby Lobby* decision itself was strictly limited to closely held organizations, but it applied entity theory to reach its holding. In doing so, the decision implied that the religious preferences or sympathies of a corporation's shareholders could be equated with the preferences and sympathies of the entity itself.

It may have been thrilling for a few legally minded Americans to debate whether partnerships were entities or aggregates in the 1910s, but by the 1990s, the Revised Uniform Partnership Act had declared that partnerships were in fact entities (and therefore legal persons, not mere aggregates).[17] The debate on this question is now closed; partnerships are essentially entities vested with personhood. And there has never been any serious debate about corporations, which have quite consistently been viewed as artificial legal persons. It is convenient, for most purposes, to treat them as such. And convenience is an acceptable social end for atheists and religiously minded individuals alike.

Proponents of religious freedom cheered for David Green, the founder of Hobby Lobby's chain of stores,[18] as he successfully resisted the full force of the U.S. government. That government had tried to force him, his family, and his company to purchase health insurance for abortifacients which, Green believed as a matter of

---

[16] *Hobby Lobby*, 134 S.Ct. at 2766.

[17] See the Revised Uniform Partnership Act § 201(a) (1994) ("A partnership is an entity distinct from its partners").

[18] Hobby Lobby was consolidated with a parallel case involving a challenge to the government's contraceptive mandate by Norman and Elizabeth Hahn and their three sons, devout members of the Mennonite Church, and a corporation named Conestoga Wood Specialties. *Hobby Lobby*, 134 S.Ct. at 2764. The Hahns individually had been dismissed as plaintiffs by the Third Circuit Court of Appeals when "it concluded that the [contraceptive] 'mandate does not impose any requirements on the Hahns in their personal capacity." *Id.* at 2765 (quoting from the Third Circuit's opinion) (citation omitted).

his Christian faith, would cause the death of unborn natural persons. Green fought back and prevailed. His religious rights were vindicated by the Supreme Court's reasoning.

3. The lack of corporate capacity to practice religion

Somewhere between the cheers for David Green and the dull parsing of the word "person" in the RFRA statutory text lie other important questions. *Should* corporations be endowed with religious freedom? How can we expect corporations to exercise that freedom? Does granting religious rights to corporations necessarily advance religion? We should consider first what a corporation is and then examine particular sorts of rights.

A corporation is not a pagan creation nor an anti-religious construction, but neither is it a religious vessel, intrinsically or otherwise. It is an intangible legal structure in which natural persons gather toward common ends. It is an organization of human wants and capital aligned among several actors, namely management and owners. It is neither good nor evil, lazy nor disciplined. It represents simply an assemblage of the aims of the natural persons behind it, and nothing more.

Like a suspension bridge, the relationship between shareholders and directors is the tension that gives the corporation structure. In a for-profit corporation, shareholders invest capital and vote for members of the board; the board wields power over the enterprise while owing duties to its investors.[19] It is a construction of great utility and potential, engineering human nature and capital toward ends that could never be accomplished by a single natural person. Indeed, the corporation might be one of the most powerful forces on the planet, even more powerful than some sovereign nations. But its parameters and powers are limited to those that we choose to permit and recognize.[20] "Put roughly, 'person' signifies what law makes it signify."[21] And what it signifies has particular import when applied to fundamental rights.

Certain fundamental rights are enshrined in the Bill of Rights, the first ten amendments to the U.S. Constitution. The right of free speech is one of them.[22] Corporations, the courts have confirmed, enjoy the same free-speech rights as natural persons.[23]

---

[19] Model Business Corporations Act 8.31(b)(1)(i) (2002) (allowing damage claims against directors who have caused damages to the corporation or its shareholders).

[20] See *Trustees of Dartmouth College,* 17 U.S. at 636 ("A corporation is an artificial being, invisible, intangible, and existing only in contemplation of law. Being the mere creature of law, it possesses only those properties which the charter of its creation confers upon it, either expressly, or as incidental to its very existence. These are such as are supposed best calculated to effect the object for which it was created.").

[21] Dewey, *supra* note 7, at 655.

[22] U.S. Const. amend. I (1791).

[23] *First National Bank of Boston v. Bellotti,* 435 U.S. 765, 784 (1978).

If a corporation publishes a newsletter, which is not simply a collection of the views of any of its individual officers or employees, that newsletter enjoys constitutional protections. In that sense, a corporation can 'speak.' Were the corporation not vested with free speech rights, certain corporate speech could be regulated or silenced by the government in ways inconsistent with the existence of the right.

Another important, fundamental right is the right to vote.[24] Additional established rights protect the privileges of adopting a child, enjoying intimacy, or marrying.[25] Yet no one would suggest that corporations should be entitled to vote, marry, or adopt children. These rights and privileges are inherently personal and only properly vested in natural persons. Thus, some rights can be exercised by an artificial person as an entity (and therefore require protection), but others cannot (and do not require protection).

What about religious exercises? It seems clear that a faith entity cannot worship – not even a church. A corporation cannot take communion, be baptized, be ordained, or receive absolution. A corporation cannot pray, fast, or observe religious dietary restrictions. It cannot be devoted to Christ; it cannot be saved (in the spiritual sense) or damned. These are inherently human activities, events, and sacraments. Fundamentally, a corporation cannot experience the Creator's love. It would therefore seem impossible for corporations, or even churches, to exercise or enjoy religious freedoms functionally as entities.

A rejoinder to this assertion should be considered.[26] "Neither can a corporation," an objector might say, "experience a deprivation of due process of law, yet the law recognizes and protects against the same."[27] Granted, a corporation is not actually a person. A for-profit corporation is really nothing more than an intersection of human interests held by management and equity stakeholders. Attaching the label of legal personhood for purposes of bestowing certain categories of rights, powers, and responsibilities on the entity is simply a convenient way of accomplish-

---

[24] U.S. Const. amend. XV (1870). "It is beyond cavil that 'voting is of the most fundamental significance under our constitutional structure'" [*Burdick v. Takushi*, 504 U.S. 428, 433 (1992), quoting *Ill. State Bd. of Elections v. Socialist Workers Party*, 440 U.S. 173, 184 (1979)].

[25] Jedd Medefind, "In Defense of the Christian Orphan Case Movement", 2 J. Christian Legal Thought 9, 14 (Spring 2012) (calling adoption "the most fundamental of needs"); but see *Browder v. Harmeyer*, 453 N.E.2d 301, 308–309 (Ind.App.1983) (holding that a grandparent with intermittent custody of her grandchild seeking to adopt had no constitutional liberty interest). See also *Loving v. Virginia*, 388 U.S. 1, 12 (1967) (viewing the right to marry as a fundamental right).

[26] See Rik Torfs, "The Internal Crisis of Religious Freedom", 4 Int'l J. of Religious Freedom, 17, 18 (2011). Torfs boldly asserts, "Reducing religious freedom to its individual aspects ... leads to dismantling all religious organisations, and denies the collective aspect of religion." It is one thing to consider religious exercise in the collective, however, and another to locate its existence and expression independent of the collective.

[27] *Covington & Lexington Turnpike Rd. Co. v. Sandford*, 164 U.S. 578, 592 (1896).

ing acceptable ends.[28] For example, a corporation is a legal person with regard to property ownership. It enjoys the efficiency of conveying an acre of dirt with the signature of a single corporate officer instead of requiring the approval of thousands of individual shareholders. A U.S. corporation is typically an independent taxpayer, collecting its receipts and deductions and presenting them on just one tax return rather than diffusing those reportable events among an evolving list of relatively disinterested owner-shareholders.[29] Furthermore, a corporation's ability to hire and fire employees ensures continuity when supervisors come and go. Moreover, endowing corporations with personhood enables governments to ask them to comply with the law and other social expectations, and to sanction them when they don't.[30]

The justifications for endowing a corporation with protection from due process deprivations or uncompensated eminent domain takings do not rest on a corporation's actual personhood, which is simply a convenient legal fiction for some purposes (such as taxation) but not for others (e.g., adoption).[31] It might be argued that corporations may exercise all but the more intensely personal freedoms, but this is an imprecise measure.[32] A more sensitive test of whether a corporation should enjoy a particular right considers whether the right resonates in an intersection of human interests found within the corporate format.[33] Particularly with for-profit faith entities, particular religious tenets cannot typically be located at the intersection of shareholder, officer, and director concerns.

4. The problem with entity personhood for religious matters

Tax-exempt status for churches rests on the religious aims and functions of the churches as entities. The unthinking application of entity-personhood theory to faith entities may thus raise unforeseen problems with regard to the recognition of

---

[28] See *Trustees of Dartmouth College v. Woodward,* 17 U.S. (4 Wheat.) 518, 636 (1819) (Marshall, C.J.) (characterizing the corporate characteristic of individuality as one that "enable[s] a corporation to manage its own affairs, and to hold property without the perplexing intricacies, the hazardous and endless necessity, of perpetual conveyances for the purpose of transmitting it from hand to hand").

[29] 26 U.S.C. § 11(a) (2016).

[30] American Law Institute, *Principles of Corporate Governance* 60 (1994).

[31] See *Trustees of Dartmouth College,* 17 U.S. at 636 (calling a corporation "an artificial being, invisible, intangible, and existing only in contemplation of law"). "A corporation is an artificial being, invisible, intangible, and existing only in contemplation of law. Being the mere creature of law, it possesses only those properties which the charter of its creation confers upon it, either expressly, or as incidental to its very existence. These are such as are supposed best calculated to effect the object for which it was created." *Id.*

[32] But see *United States v. White,* 322 U.S. 694, 698–699 (1944) (denying corporations the privilege against self-incrimination because it is a "purely personal" right).

[33] Cf. Frank Michelman, "Property, Utility, and Fairness: Comments on the Ethical Foundations of "Just Compensation" Law", 80 Harv. L. Rev. 1165, 1223 (1967) (calling for a legal conclusion upon the occurrence of a "distinctly perceived, sharply crystallized, investment-backed expectation").

religious freedoms. Endowing churches with entity-personhood would empower taxing authorities and enhance their ability to shape what happens in churches. It would legitimize taxing authorities' oversight of the words spoken by the faithful.

In 2004, just days before the U.S. presidential election between George W. Bush and challenger John Kerry, a minister at a Pasadena, California church delivered a sermon titled "If Jesus Debated President Bush and Senator Kerry." The sermon precipitated a chain of events that ultimately endangered the church's tax-exempt status.[34] Similar situations have played out in settings across the United States.[35]

The U.S. Internal Revenue Service (IRS) monitors the political activity of religious organizations that enjoy tax-exempt status.[36] An example from an official IRS publication describes a factual scenario in which a church could lose its tax-exempt status:

> Minister D is the minister of Church M, a Section 501(c)(3) organization. During regular services of Church M shortly before the election, Minister D preached on a number of issues, including the importance of voting in the upcoming election, and concluded by stating, "It is important that you all do your duty in the election and vote for Candidate W." Because Minister D's remarks indicating support for Candidate W were made during an official church service, they constitute political campaign intervention by Church M.[37]

Implicit in this example is the construction of Church M pursuant to an aggressive application of entity theory. Note how the spoken words of one church member (the minister) are linked to the church as an entity. The IRS effortlessly yokes the pastor's words to the church, as opposed to construing them as simply representing the political opinions of one member of the aggregate. Minister D is actually speaking to an aggregate, not as (or on behalf of) an entity. But the IRS views the minister's words as corporate words. As such, the IRS is tacitly applying entity theory to the act of worship.

This mistaken IRS view of religious services could be traced to the same fault lines that underlie the *Hobby Lobby* decision: a misapplication of the entity theory to religious practices. The IRS's thinking in its Publication 1828 is based on the assumption that the political text within the sermon was essentially spoken by the

---

[34] Keith S. Blair, "Praying for a Tax Break: Churches, Political Speech, and the Loss of 501(c)(3) Tax Exempt Status", 86 Denv. U. L. Rev. 405, 406 (2009).

[35] *Id.*

[36] Internal Revenue Service, U.S. Department of the Treasury, Pub. 1828, *Tax Guide for Churches and Religious Organizations* 8 (rev. 2015), available at https://www.irs.gov/pub/irs-pdf/p1828.pdf.

[37] *Id.*

church as a corporate entity.[38] As a result, the IRS considers it appropriate to threaten or even withdraw the church's tax-exempt status in such an instance.[39]

A more accurate understanding of worship in the aggregate might reach a different conclusion, namely that the minister's preaching is one voice inspiring the congregation. The congregation does not worship through the minister; it worships as a collection of individuals assembled in a sacred place. Viewed in this aggregate light, the minister's message ought not to stain the church's tax-exempt status, the loss of which could be catastrophic to the church's operations. Unless the political activity is clearly a corporate act (such as if the church's board of trustees has formally endorsed it), a pastor's exhortations to vote in a particular way ought not to be characterized as campaign interventions by the church as an entity.

The power to tax is the power to destroy – and the power to persecute.[40] The IRS's power to withdraw tax-exempt status from churches or other nonprofit faith entities is a potentially destructive scope of authority. Quite possibly, the direction of persecution against faith entities in future years will originate from this power to tax, as governments suspend tax exemptions because of the 'political' acts of churches. The IRS and other taxing authorities will be empowered in any concerted effort to withdraw tax exemptions from churches by the very doctrine at the center of the *Hobby Lobby* decision – entity personhood.

Honesty and accuracy about the way things really are is important, especially when it comes to witnessing about matters of faith. Religiously minded individuals should be accurate in depicting their own worship. A church, as a corporate entity, does not worship any more than it can adopt a child, adhere to a faith commitment, or vote for a political candidate. A church is organized with the aim of creating a platform for worship, but the exercise of religious faith itself occurs in and only in the aggregate.[41] The accuracy of this depiction becomes even more forceful when

---

[38] See also Kim Colby, "Practical Steps That Religious Institutions Should Consider in the Post-Obergefell World", 11 The Christian Lawyer 19, 24 (Dec. 2015) (noting that during oral arguments in the Obergefell case, Justice Alito asked the Solicitor General whether religious schools prohibiting same-sex conduct among students would lose their tax-exempt status, to which the reply was that that might well be an issue).

[39] Too much lobbying can jeopardize a nonprofit entity's tax-exempt status, as can any degree of participation in a political campaign. See 26 U.S.C. § 501(h) (lobbying); 501(c)(3) (political campaign intervention).

[40] *M'Culloch v. State,* 17 U.S. 316, 327 (1819) (Marshall, J.): "An unlimited power to tax involves, necessarily, a power to destroy; because there is a limit beyond which no institution and no property can bear taxation."

[41] In the Christian tradition, Paul's letters speak about the importance of the church, and both 1 Corinthians and Romans speak of the unity of the body of Christ. Paul seems to espouse the equivalent of entity theory when he speaks of the oneness of the experience of the Eucharist: "We, who are many, are one bread, one body; for we all partake of the one bread" (1 Cor 10:17). He also says, "For as the body is one, and hath many members, and all the members of the body, being many, are one body; so

the organization involved is a for-profit faith entity such as Hobby Lobby, which engages in the retail sale of craft supplies as its main enterprise while only incidentally abiding by Christian precepts, such as closing on Sundays.

The place for individual faith is the individual, not in corporations. The place for religion within a church is with its aggregate worshippers. Churches and other faith entities "minister to their parishioners, run food banks, distribute food, offer job counseling and, generally, deliver services to the community at large."[42] However, churches themselves do not worship, practice religion, seek forgiveness, or enter into communion with God. These practices are reserved for natural persons, not artificial ones.

5. Conclusion

"All things are lawful; but not all things edify," Paul wrote (1 Cor 10:23). He meant, in one sense, that just because we *can* do something doesn't mean that we *should* do it. For him, the ends should not justify the means. Hobby Lobby owner David Green's victory over a bullying government – preserving his integrity against a Rome that gave no quarter to his faith – represents an inspirational outcome, a happy end. But the path by which that victory was attained was paved with a false assertion, namely the assertion that corporations can enjoy religious freedoms. This foundation can only degrade with use, and with that degradation may come enhanced persecution of faith entities by taxing authorities. Tactically speaking, the means by which *Hobby Lobby* was won may, in the long run, jeopardize religious liberties. This will not do. We should reclaim religious freedoms as non-corporate matters of conviction.

Religion's place is in the devout human heart, in the gatherings of worshippers in the aggregate, and in the worshippers themselves. It is not in a corporation, nor does it lie within any sort of artificial legal entity, a creature of law that even the law calls a fiction and a construction of convenience. Religion's place is not in a company, but in us. To pretend otherwise is dishonest, inaccurate, and potentially dangerous, as it may prove to exchange a short-term tactical victory for a strategic long-term defeat.

---

also is Christ. For in one Spirit were we all baptized into one body" (1 Cor 12:12). In Romans he adds, "For even as we have many members in one body, and all the members have not the same office: so we, who are many, are one body in Christ, and severally members one of another" (Rom 12:4-5). Consider also the line from Peter Scholtes's 1960s hymn "They'll Know We Are Christians by Our Love," in which he wrote, "We are one in the Spirit, we are one in the Lord." Pauline texts could be read as lending support to the *Hobby Lobby* court's view of religious exercise through a united corporate entity, but I think Paul is speaking of the oneness of communion with the Holy Spirit, not a oneness of faith, for in 1 Corinthians 12 he continues, "Now there are diversities of gifts, but the same Spirit. And there are diversities of ministrations, and the same Lord. And there are diversities of workings, but the same God, who worketh things in all" (1 Cor 12:4-6).

[42] Blair, *supra* note 45, at 406.

Noteworthy

The noteworthy items are structured in two groups: annual reports and global surveys, regional and country reports, and specific issues. Though we apply serious criteria in the selection of items noted, it is beyond our capacity to scrutinize the accuracy of every statement made. We therefore disclaim responsibility for the contents of the items noted. The compilation was produced by Janet Epp Buckingham.

Annual reports and global surveys

World Watch List: Where Faith Costs the Most
Open Doors, USA, January 2015

https://www.opendoorsusa.org/christian-persecution/stories/the-2015-world-watch-list-unveiled/ The World Watch List (WWL) represents the 50 countries where persecution of Christians is the worst and is compiled from a specially designed questionnaire of 50 questions covering various aspects of religious freedom. In the number-one spot is North Korea.

International Religious Freedom Report for 2015
US Department of State, 2015

https://2009-2017.state.gov/j/drl/rls/irf/religiousfreedom/index.htm

The US Department of State produces a comprehensive annual report on international religious freedom.

2015 Annual Report

European Parliament Intergroup, EU, June 2016 http://www.religiousfreedom.eu/2016/06/30/annual-report-on-the-state-of-freedom-of-religion-or-belief-in-the-world-2015-2016/

The European Parliament Intergroup on Freedom of Religion or Belief and Religious Intolerance released its second annual report on freedom of religion or belief around the world.

United Nations Special Rapporteur Reports

Special Rapporteur on freedom of religion or belief, Heiner Bielefeldt, December 2014 https://www.ohchr.org/EN/Issues/FreedomReligion/Pages/Annual.aspx

The UN Special Rapporteur on freedom of religion or belief issued a report, A/HRC/28/66, that focused on violence committed "in the name of religion."

Special Rapporteur on freedom of religion or belief,
Heiner Bielefeldt, August 2015

https://www.un.org/en/ga/search/view_doc.asp?symbol=A/70/286

The UN Special Rapporteur on freedom of religion or belief issued an interim report, A/70/286, that focused on the rights of the child and his or her parents in the area of freedom of religion or belief.

Regional and Country Reports

Genocide against Christians in the Middle East

Knights of Columbus and In Defense of Christians, March 2016; 278 pages

This document, submitted to US Secretary of State John Kerry, is a comprehensive, well-documented report on Christians who were murdered, attacked or displaced in the Middle East.

IIRF Publishes Report on Discrimination of Armenians in Turkey
International Institute for Religious Freedom, April 2015

https://www.iirf.eu/journal-books/iirf-reports-english/iirf-reports-2015-2/

The IIRF published a report on discrimination faced by Armenians in Turkey titled, "The Armenian Question in Turkey's Domestic and International Policy." The report is authored by Prof Dr Dr Thomas Schirrmacher.

Special issues

The Ultimate Guide to Internet Censorship
WizCase

https://www.wizcase.com/blog/ultimate-guide-internet-censorship/

This is a helpful guide to Internet censorship, which has been used to remove Christian content in some parts of the world. The guide includes concrete actions to combat censorship.

IPPFORB established

International Panel of Parliamentarians for Freedom of Religion or Belief, 19 September 2015

Parliamentarians in attendance at the September 2015 New York Conference titled Multinational Efforts to Strengthen Freedom of Religion or Belief, signed a "Resolution for Freedom of Religion or Belief." This resolution forms the basis for IPPFORB, an international network of Parliamentarians committed to working towards freedom of religion and belief. www.ippforb.com

Documentation

IPPFORB Conference, New York, 2015: Resolution for Freedom of Religion or Belief

Cognizant that severe violations of freedom of religion or belief continue to occur around the world, perpetrated by states, state proxies, and non-state actors;

Taking note of studies indicating an increase in restrictions on the free practice of religion or belief, with the majority of the global population living in countries where their freedom to peacefully practice their faith could be or is restricted;

Whereas in response to these violations, a group of parliamentarians gathered in Oxford, England, in June 2014 to discuss ways to confront the abuses;

Recalling that at the Nobel Peace Center in Oslo, Norway, parliamentarians from around the world gathered in November 2014 to pledge to advance religious freedom for all and launched the International Panel of Parliamentarians for Freedom of Religion or Belief;

Reaffirming the Charter for Freedom of Religion or Belief signed in Oslo that commits parliamentarians to support Article 18 of the Universal Declaration of Human Rights, including the right of individuals to hold or not to hold any faith or belief, to change belief, to be free from coercion to adopt a different belief, and to peacefully practice the faith of their choice alone or in community with others;

Welcoming the creation of panels in domestic parliaments since the Oslo meeting, including in Brazil, Norway, and Pakistan, and existing bipartisan caucuses in Canada, the European Parliament, the United Kingdom, and the United States;

Taking note of and welcoming the creation of the International Contact Group for Freedom of Religion or Belief networking likeminded governments committed to advancing freedom of religion or belief around the world;

Appreciating the critically important work of civil society organizations, religious leaders, and individuals in academia who are endeavoring to advance freedom of religion or belief with their communities of influence and societies at large;

Now, in New York, on 19 September 2015, the International Panel of Parliamentarians for Freedom of Religion or Belief *commit to pursue efforts* that:

Advocate for individuals suffering from persecution because of their religious or other forms of belief and urge greater respect for freedom of religion or belief;

Strengthen and promote freedom of thought, conscience, religion and belief as a universal, established and non-derogable human right, as set out in the Universal Declaration, in international customary law and treaties, and in the work of national, regional, and global agencies and political bodies;

Enhance global cooperation by working across geographical, political, and religious lines to mobilize effective responses through regular communications, sharing of information, and endeavoring to meet annually;

Expand the network of parliaments focused on freedom of religion or belief around the world by supporting the creation of new parliamentary platforms or groups that support Article 18 and that are politically and religiously diverse;

Build capacity among parliamentarians committed to advancing religious freedom, both for those in stable countries and those in countries with problematic records on freedom of religion or belief, so as to equip parliamentarians to advocate for change at home and abroad;

Increase the number of governments and international institutions responding to the growing crisis of persecution of believers and non-believers and encourage the commitment of increased resources to ensure greater respect for this fundamental freedom; and

Build stronger linkages between members of parliament and civil society organizations, religious leaders, and members of academia so as to find more impactful ways to advance freedom of religion or belief globally.

Signed by Parliamentarians in attendance at the September, 2015 New York Conference, "Multinational Efforts to Strengthen Freedom of Religion or Belief".

Editors' note: As this resolution cannot be found on the website www.ippforb.com, it is documented here.

Guidlines for authors can be found at
www.iirf.eu/index.php?id=30

Review Article

Islamic Discourses on Accusations of Unbelief and Apostasy

Carsten Polanz[1]

Accusations of Unbelief: A Diachronic Perspective on Takfir
Camilla Adang (ed.)

Leiden/Boston: Brill, 2015, 534 pp., ISBN 9789004304734, ISBN 9004304738, € 175.00, US$ 234.00.

"Let There Be No Compulsion in Religion" (Sura 2:256): Apostasy from Islam as Judged by Contemporary Islamic Theologians
Christine Schirrmacher

Bonn: Verlag für Kultur und Wissenschaft, 2015; Eugene, OR: Wipf & Stock, 2016, 620 pp., ISBN 978-3-86269-114-2; ISBN 9781498291538, € 49.80, US$ 56.00 (Web Price).

The Muslim world is torn by numerous internal disputes. These battles are by no means limited to the age-old conflict between Sunnis and Shias, which is currently being carried on mainly by Saudi Arabia and Iran through proxy wars in such places as Syria, Iraq and Yemen. Even within the two great Muslim confessional communities, the issue of what constitutes 'genuine' Islam often leads to bloody feuds.

The historical origins and contemporary grounds for this growing phenomenon of intra-Islamic heresy charges and the closely related topic of the lack of public freedom of opinion and religion, including freedom to change one's religion, in Muslim-majority societies are the topic of both Adang's omnibus volume and Christine Schirrmacher's habilitation treatise.

Fuelling this debate is the concept of *takfir* (derived from *kafir* = unbeliever, infidel), which can be rendered as excommunication or as branding as a heretic. The invocation of *takfir* implies accusing fellow Muslims of unbelief on the grounds that they have crossed a red line by holding ideas contrary to fundamental points of Islamic doctrine or politically inacceptable views.

---

[1] Carsten Polanz is lecturer in Islamic Studies at Giessen School of Theology, Germany, research fellow at the International Institute of Islamic Studies in Bonn, and editor-in-chief of its bilingual periodical Islam and Christianity.

This kind of charge can have serious consequences, since the prevailing opinion of all major schools of jurisprudence is that apostasy from Islam is a capital offence. Even where the death penalty is not in fact applied, those found guilty of *takfir* may lose their employment or be rejected by society, expelled from the family or divorced. The accused person's writings may be banned, burned or attacked in polemic rebuttals. Even when they are ultimately pronounced not guilty, the personal and social costs for the accused can be enormous (Adang, 14–15).

1. The historical roots of the *takfir* problem

In the introductory essay to her omnibus volume (pp. 1–24), Camilla Adang, Professor of Islamic Studies at Tel Aviv University, demonstrates that curses and heresy charges against individuals or distinct groups are not just a recent phenomenon; rather, their roots lie deep in the history of Islam, reaching right back to the Koran itself. At the same time, some early Islamic scholars warned – also on the basis of the Koran, the Islamic tradition of Muhammad's habits (the *sunna*), and specific statements in Hadith literature, with particular stress on the example of the fourth Caliph Ali – against making overly hasty or ill-considered accusations of unbelief against fellow believers who held differing opinions.

According to one tradition, anyone who falsely accuses his brother of unbelief makes himself an unbeliever. Clearly, in this instance the traditional literature reflects an increasing tendency towards mutual malediction in the struggles for supremacy after Muhammad's death. From the start – even in the later phase of Muhammad's life in Medina – the issue of truth was never separated from the question of power, with the result that differences of opinion on central matters of faith tended to be resolved by violence.

Adang notes that legal treatises, not theological ones, were pre-eminent in addressing the necessary conditions for membership in the Islamic community. Here one finds detailed classifications of the various forms of unbelief, apostasy, heresy, calumny and blasphemy. As there is no consensus on definitions, nor clear demarcations between the differing concepts, there is a great danger that individual groups may pour oil on the flames of existing intimidation and mistrust within Islam by setting up their own definitions and delineating the circle of true believers ever more closely. This threat is even greater since Islam, unlike for instance the Roman Catholic Church, has no authoritative central institution to make decisions binding on all sections of the community.

2. The question of an indispensable minimum standard of belief

Very early on, the authenticity of believers' profession became a fundamental matter of debate: should it be left to Allah to adjudicate in the hereafter and should the community simply brand offenders as sacrilegious sinners, or should believers be expected to demonstrate the genuineness of their commitment in this world by deeds of piety or by specific political convictions or actions? Groups such as the so-called Khawarij (or Kharijites), regarded by experts as the forerunners of today's jihadists, developed a minimalist concept of the community of believers, and all who failed to identify with their specific politico-religious ideology in both word and deed were declared unbelievers. Appealing to the Prophet's example, they propagated the idea of emigrating to an isolated region from which they could later launch attacks on the "unbelieving" or "apostate" Muslims.

The mainstream view in Sunni Islam today is that it is sufficient to repeat the twofold profession of Allah's uniqueness and Muhammad as his Prophet to be considered a Muslim, as long as there is no unequivocal or patent evidence of unbelief. At the same time, every Muslim is naturally expected not to publicly call into doubt belief in the other prophets and messengers, angels, the books of Allah or the resurrection and the last judgment. Many scholars would regard the acknowledgement and consistent practice of fundamental duties, such as ritual prayers, as a necessary visible sign of Muslim piety (see Robert Gleave's article in Adang, 413–433). As a rule, most scholars insist that it is the responsibility of rulers to mete out punishment and that only scholars, as "heirs of the Prophet" and "guardians of the faith," are entitled to pronounce a person apostate. Furthermore, such a pronouncement must be based on clear evidence, and the accused must be aware of their wrongdoing and must not have acted under compulsion. In certain cases, a period of opportunity for repentance must be granted.

3. The struggle for supremacy in Islamic interpretation

Along with a thorough introduction of the subject of *takfir*, Adang's volume contains 19 articles arranged in four parts, covering early Islam (7th to 10th century), the classical and post-classical period (11th to 18th century), the modern period, and finally a number of chronologically overlapping issues. The individual contributions reflect the diversity of topics on which conflicts have raged within Islam – from the relationship between sovereign divine omnipotence and human responsibility and freedom of will (see Steven Judd's article amongst others) or the familiar debate as to whether the Koran constitutes Allah's created or uncreated word.

István T. Kristó-Nagy (56–81) points out how sharply orthodox Muslims reacted when they perceived the threat posed by dualistic tendencies to the central Islamic doctrine of Allah's oneness and uniqueness (*tauhid*).

Hossein Modarressi (395–412) examines a Hadith that opens the door of paradise to all who believe in Allah's uniqueness and considers how, over the years, both Sunni and Shia scholars have added further conditions to the traditional text, so as to exclude from the community of true believers those who reject specific theological, judicial or historical convictions of their own confession.

Zoltan Szombathy (465–487) shows how differently alleged expressions of unbelief in literature can be judged. He examines especially the issue of the legal relevance of authorial intention, hotly debated among legal scholars. In the case of the Iranian writer Salman Rushdie (born 1947) and his book *The Satanic Verses*, the Egyptian grand mufti Muhammad Sayyid Tantawi (1928–2010) criticized Khomeini's apostasy fatwa specifically on the grounds that the intention behind Rushdie's allegedly blasphemous utterances had not been examined. Szombathy insists that in Great Britain, Muslim supporters of the death penalty appealed less to Rushdie's novel as evidence of his blasphemous and Islamophobic intent than to his subsequent unequivocal utterances in interviews and articles.

4. The interplay of religious and political authority

The various essays give impressive evidence that *takfir* proceedings and their incalculable impact, considerably complicated by the fact that Sharia law has never been codified, are intimately related to the dominant local social and political context. One particular strength of Adang's compendium is its investigation of the micro-history of *takfir* – that is, its contextual framework – via records of court proceedings, historical chronicles, works of literature and (in more recent cases) testimonies of private encounters and conversations.

In his article on the Hanafite classification of defamation and blasphemy as infringements of "Allah's rights" (*huquq allah*) and offences against "public values," Intisar A. Rabb (434–464) demonstrates that in most such cases in the medieval Muslim world the issue was violation of rules of social decency that had often developed centuries after the birth of Islam. Brian J. Didier's contribution (273–303) shows how a debate between local Sunni scholars and the Sufi Shamsiya community on the South Indian island of Androth arose not so much over major differences in matters of faith and practice but because of the scholars' growing intolerance towards the community. Didier interprets this behaviour as a reaction to the worldwide modern crisis of religious authority, as a result of which scholars no longer enjoy the self-evident privilege of defining what constitutes genuine Islam.

The combination of religious, political and judicial factors also played a role in heresy trials of three women's rights activists in Jordan, Kuwait and Egypt. Roswitha Badry (354–380) outlines the three women's official stands against the political instrumentalization of religion, moral double standards and sexual and domestic violence. Undeterred by personal smear campaigns against them, the women went on a counter-attack. Badry interprets their arguments as a search for an individualistic approach to Islamic texts, one that would reduce the core of Islam to a general belief in God and a spirit of justice, freedom, gender equality and love. Recent developments in the Arab world cause the author to doubt that such social movements will be able to prevail over *takfir* campaigns in the near future.

5. *Takfir* against Western democracy and its advocates

Analysing jihad and Salafist movements, Joas Wagemakers (327–353) demonstrates that *takfir* can be used to brand democratic governments as a "religion of the infidel West." Democracy is equated with unbelief because it declares the people and not Allah to be the fountainhead of legislative power and propagates ideals of human liberty and equality that are incompatible with the Koran. Such movements categorically reject moderate Muslims' attempts to legitimize certain aspects of democracy with an appeal to the primitive Islamic principle of the ruler's consultation (*shura*). Wagemakers nevertheless regards Salafist positions as determined to some extent by the social and political context, as evidenced by the fact that in countries such as Jordan, with a relatively long tradition of parliamentary elections, the Salafists tend to be less uncompromising than in Iraq, where the recent democratic process is much more closely associated with Western intervention and Shiite privilege.

6. Apostasy and its consequences in the Western context

Göran Larsson (381–392) shows how the unsettled question of apostasy and its as yet little-researched consequences for Western Muslims can influence the image of Islam and intensify anti-Muslim sentiments. He examines the case of a group of Somali converts from Islam to Christianity and analyses the social debate triggered by media reports of the aggressive reactions by some Muslims to an evangelistic rally that these Somalis held in a multi-ethnic suburb of Stockholm. Since freedom of religion and the right to change one's religion are fundamental human rights in an open and democratic society, Larsson emphasizes in his conclusion the urgent need for research into and documentation of the extent of the threat of persecution against ex-Muslims in Western societies.

7. *Anti-takfir* conferences

In the conclusion of her introduction, Adang reports on various international conferences to combat increasing jihad and takfir aggression, including the 2005 Amman conference of over 200 scholars summoned by the king of Jordan. In their so-called "Amman Message," the participants stipulated that anyone who follows one of the four Sunni schools of law (the Ja'fari, Zaydi, Ibadi and Zahiri schools) and anyone who accepts the foundational beliefs of Islam, practises its five pillars and does not deny any essential element of the faith must be considered a Muslim.

They declared that the life, honour and possessions of such people must be protected and that they may not be placed under a curse or the ban. The only country to have implemented these provisions in national legislation thus far is Tunisia (in January 2014).

Adang underscores the conspicuous reticence of Muslim scholars (especially those of the Egyptian Al-Azhar University) to publicly condemn Islamic State, even though IS has declared all who fail to join them to be infidels. In this context, the scholars appeal to warnings against reciprocal excommunication. The Al-Azhar argument is especially significant since in the past the same institution has not hesitated to pronounce accusations of infidelity against liberal and pro-Western thinkers. In fact, it has taken the lead in *takfir* trials against Egyptian intellectuals such as the literary critic Nasr Hamid Abu Zaid (1943–2010) or the philosophers Taha Husain (1889–1973) and Hasan Hanafi (born 1935). These inner contradictions may explain why – as Adang notes – counter-initiatives by Arabic and Iranian scholars have thus far borne little fruit. It appears probable that the *takfir* phenomenon will remain an integral part of Muslim society for the foreseeable future.

8. The cultural influence of pioneer religious and political thinkers

At this point, the question arises as to who might be capable of fostering a fundamental change or, conversely, who is impeding a profound self-critical analysis of the theological breeding ground of mutual cursing and persecution of different-minded people. This question is the basis of Christine Schirrmacher's work, published in both German and English. Schirrmacher, currently professor of Islamic studies at Friedrich Wilhelm University in Bonn and the Evangelische Theologische Faculteit in Leuven, Belgium, investigates the role played by leaders of religious opinion in creating the social and intellectual climate in Muslim-majority countries. To what extent do they legitimize the treatment of Muslims who become Christians, atheists or members of an unrecognized Islamic minority as the most heinous sinners, a shame for their family, enemies of Allah and traitors to the Muslim community? To what extent do they justify the discrimination, persecution and death threats that such people endure?

In her introduction, Schirrmacher points out the contradiction between the largely secular criminal law in most Muslim countries and the clause in many constitutions stating that Islam is the state religion and the Sharia the sole or main source of legislation. Conservative scholars appeal to the latter provisions when they demand a more stringent application of Sharia, which provides for capital punishment for those who change their religion. This requirement is based less on the relevant verses of the Koran than on widely accepted Hadiths. In practice, the conflict between secular law and the implicit affirmation of Sharia creates a broad area of legal and personal uncertainty for Muslims who do not belong to the mainstream or who abandon Islam.

Schirrmacher compares the views of three Islamic scholars of the 20th and 21st centuries, all with international influence and writing in various languages, each of whom has published a monograph and numerous articles on the topics of apostasy and religious liberty.

9. The radical position of Abu al-Ala Maududi

Schirrmacher presents the Indo-Pakistani scholar Abu al-Ala Maududi (1903–1979) as a pioneer of a hard line against any kind of divergence from Islam. In his innumerable writings, he indefatigably propagated the total ideology of an all-embracing Islamic Sharia state (including criminal law). Through his political advocacy, he decisively stamped his influence on Pakistani society and its constitution (consider the country's increasingly strict blasphemy laws). Maududi regarded the mere existence of apostates as a threat to the state, which he was convinced ought to be co-terminous with the fellowship of the faithful. Importantly, however, he offered no answers to practical questions such as what authority should be responsible for deciding who is an apostate, pronouncing convictions and carrying out executions.

Echoing the title of a book by the Armenian writer Hrant Dink, Schirrmacher shows how the seed sown by Maududi's speeches and writings and the activity of his Jammati Islami group have borne fruit in contemporary Pakistan and elsewhere. Instead of proposing concrete solutions and forward-looking answers to the issue of Pakistan's identity, Maududi's black-and-white approach prepared the ideological ground for the recent, ever-increasing dynamic of intolerance, exclusion, persecution and violence directed at Christians, Ahmadiyya followers, other minorities and anyone critical of Islam. Even though no executions have taken place yet under Pakistan's anti-blasphemy laws, a mere accusation can result in social isolation, family threats, confinement, criminal charges, violence and abuse, both in prison or after release – even if one is cleared of all charges. Anyone who, like the late Minister for Religious Affairs Shahbaz Bhatti (murdered in 2011), speaks out against the blasphemy laws becomes the target of militant Islamists. The precarious situation for minorities is exacerbated by police indifference, passivity of the courts, and politicians who arbitrarily abuse their position (see Schirrmacher, 503 and 552ff).

10. Abdullah Saeed as an advocate of complete freedom of religion

The opposite end of the spectrum is represented by Abdullah Saeed, professor of Arabic and Islamic studies at Melbourne University. Born in 1960 on the Maldive Islands, Saeed studied Islamic theology in Saudi Arabia and Pakistan. Seeking an Islamic justification for wide-ranging religious liberty, he calls into question not only the credibility and/or current interpretation of the pertinent traditions but also the fusion of state and religion that is so dear to Islamists. Saeed sees this fusion as a product of particular social and political conditions in the 7th-century Arab peninsula. He thus focusses especially on the early and pacific statements of the Koran that derive from Muhammad's Meccan period.

Unlike the vast majority of past and present legal scholars, Saeed refuses to relativize the famous affirmation of Sura 2:256 that there should be no compulsion in religion in favour of public Islamic supremacy. Although his attempt to harmonize Islamic texts with the principles of modern freedom-loving democratic societies may not offer an all-embracing and coherent alternative for the interpretation and application of primary Islamic sources, Schirrmacher highlights the positive effect of such a courageous and unambiguous stance for religious liberty and against the timeless validity of the Sharia. It is most unfortunate that Saeed's activity has thus far been confined to the periphery of the Muslim world and that his theses, delivered primarily in English at conferences in the West, have found scarcely any echo among Arab World theologians (Schirrmacher, 398–399).

11. The middle path of Yusuf al-Qaradawi

Between Maududi and Saeed is the most widely held view of Muslim scholars, exemplified for Schirrmacher by the extremely influential Egyptian scholar and television preacher Yusuf al-Qaradawi (born 1926). His presence in television and internet, financed mainly by his sponsors in Qatar, his over 150 books (some published worldwide in multiple languages) and his leading role in international scholarly networks, makes him one of the most influential present-day Sunni scholars.

What al-Qaradawi regards as a balanced and genuinely Islamic middle path (called Wasatiyya) provides for no criminal sanction for those who abandon Islam, other than the Koranic threat of infernal punishment in the afterlife. A different picture emerges in the case of what he denotes as "major apostasy," where one openly expresses doubts as to the fundamental teachings of Islam (which al-Qaradawi regards as beyond question) or the timeless validity of the Sharia. Such "major" forms of infidelity and apostasy qualify as political crimes and treason against the community, and in the light of Islamic criminal procedures such as the prohibition of private justice, they call for capital punishment, lest individual apostasy become collective (Schirrmacher, 236ff).

12. Indirect legitimization of violence

As Schirrmacher's analysis convincingly shows, al-Qaradawi's position represents no meaningful progress, since individuals are still prohibited from drawing any public or socially effective consequences from their private convictions. However moderate he may be in contrast to radical groups, al-Qaradawi's ideology maintains a close link between truth claims and power. He and allied groups thus continue to contribute to the atmosphere of suspicion and censorship about which they themselves so passionately complain when their own position is under threat. They do desist, as a rule, from explicitly labelling individuals as heretics, and they oppose exaggerated and unthinking accusations of unbelief, especially by unqualified lay persons (which most leaders of jihad happen to be), as imperilling Islamic unity, social stability and the projected image of Islam as a religion of peace and tolerance. Nevertheless, their books and sermons furnish a pattern of thought (e.g. "whoever calls in question the timeless validity of the Sharia is guilty of apostasy") on which more radical groups base their actions. The most striking example of such indirect justification of violence is the defence offered by the al-Azhar scholar Muhammad al-Ghazali (1917–1996), also closely linked to al-Qaradawi's Wasatiyya movement, who defended the attacker of Faraj Fauda, a secular opponent of Sharia, in court by arguing that he had done only what the state should have done long ago (Schirrmacher, 120–123).

13. The urgent need for fresh thinking in Islam

The magnitude of the problem is highlighted by a 2010 Pew Research Center study, which found that 62% of Egyptians, 61% of Jordanians and 64% of Pakistanis were in favour of the death penalty for apostasy. In this context, Schirrmacher's study is extremely timely and relevant to the European situation, in which established mosque associations look to seemingly moderate authorities such as al-Qaradawi for guidance as they seek to live as far as possible in conformity with the Sharia in the Western diaspora and as they envision a step-by-step Islamization of European societies. In her conclusion, Schirrmacher emphasizes that Islamists such as Maududi and al-Qaradawi often enjoy greater opportunities to spread their ideology through book markets, mosques and modern media than the minority group, such as Abdullah Saeed, who champion full freedom of religion.

It is time for Europe to engage seriously with the lack of freedom of religion and opinion in the Muslim world. To do so, Europeans must gain a deeper understanding of the spreading *takfir* phenomenon and the interrelated personal, religious, political and even economic motives and interests involved in the ongoing intra-Islamic debates. Both volumes reviewed here make it abundantly clear that without a basic reorientation of Islamic theology and jurisprudence and a readiness to relativize the inviolability of the Koran, Muhammad's example and the historical consensus of legal experts on the issue of apostasy, there is no hope for a permanent and fundamental end to violence and oppression, nor for any genuine strengthening of civil society and the essential, concomitant freedom of religion and opinion.

Christine Schirrmacher

"Let there be no Compulsion in Religion" (Sura 2:256)

Apostasy from Islam as judged by
contemporary Islamic Theologians

Discourses on
Apostasy,
Religious Freedom,
and Human Rights

Book Reviews

Ethnische "Säuberungen" in der Moderne: Globale Wechselwirkungen nationalistischer und rassistischer Gewaltpolitik im 19. und 20. Jahrhundert (Ethnic "Cleansing" in Modern Times: Global interactions of nationalist and racist policies of violence in the 19th and 20th centuries)
Michael Schwartz

Munich: Oldenbourg Verlag, 2013, 697 pp., hardcover, ISBN 9783486704259, € 74.95, pbk., ISBN 9783110485134, € 34.95.

Michael Schwartz, an assistant professor at the Institute of Contemporary History in Munich-Berlin and a private lecturer at Münster University in recent and modern history, has written a classic on a disturbing topic which should stir all free states around the world. As the book jacket rightly observes:

> Ethnic "cleansings" are the dark side of our modern democratization and nation-building. As early as the 19th century, the Balkans and the non-European colonies developed into locations where this form of problem resolution was learned. Beginning in 1914, these techniques of violence came back to hit Europe. In both of the World Wars, their destructive power exceeded everything that anyone could have imagined. Since that time, developments in the world have been shaped by ethnic "cleansings" – from Palestine, India/Pakistan all the way to Rwanda, where in the past there would have been peaceful alternatives. Michael Schwartz describes the global connections and showcases the shocking diversity of examples of acts of ethnic violence in our modern world. This difficulty has never been presented with more urgency and dedication.

Ethnic "cleansing" means the removal of an ethnic, national or religious group from a certain territory. It can occur through violent displacement, resettlement, population exchange, deportation or murder. The term emerged during the wars in Yugoslavia in 1992 as a loan translation from Serbian *(etničko čišćenje)* and has become established in international usage over the past decade. According to Schwartz, "cleansing" should always be in quotation marks since it is a euphemistic expression used by the perpetrator.

Of course, the term designates a much older practice. Ethnic "cleansing" is in a certain sense a broader term for genocide, which represents the worst but not the sole form of such action.

The victims of ethnic "cleansing" often belong to a party (for instance, an ethnic or religious group) which has its own wings that also use violence. Indeed, for example, in a planned population exchange, the perpetrators and victims in one region may have the opposite roles in another region. Or if a shift in the distribution of power occurs, revenge motivations can result in perpetrators and victims exchanging roles.

Schwartz's central thesis is that ethnic "cleansings" are unthinkable without the context of the modern West. They are closely linked with the emergence of modern nation-states and with nationalism as a legitimization of modern states (6). For Schwartz, deportations and the displacement of people groups are the dark side of the building of nation-states. His book successfully places this thesis in a global context, describing ethnic "cleansings" as the signature of modernity: "The formation of ethnically homogeneous states has not been a natural development and in no case a peaceful development. Rather, it has been a violent process which has not been concluded." (6)

Schwartz grants that there were earlier ethnic "cleansings" (7), such as the banishment of Muslims from Spain in the 17th century. This was the point when ethnic "cleansings" gradually began to replace religious "cleansings." But present-day Europe, according to Schwartz, actually did not begin until the Serbian and Greek revolts of 1804 und 1821, when the modern nationalism of Western and Central Europe leapt over to Eastern Europe (6). This, he says, is where one finds the final transition from religious to ethnic "cleansing" (9). If in 1555 the saying was *cuius regio eius religio* (who rules the region decides on the religion), beginning in the 19th century it was *cuius regio eius natio* (who rules the region decides on the nation). In 1555, those who had the wrong religious affiliation had to emigrate – if they were not killed first; 250 years later, the same approach was applied to people of the wrong ethnic background.

Edward H. Carr (1945) described ethnic "cleansings" as a consequence of the 1789 French Revolution. That is when massive sacrifices of human life were taken for granted and accepted in the name of nationalism. Such instances of genocide and ethnic "cleansings" are inconceivable without the modern administrative state. This idea has been primarily defended by Zygmunt Bauman (in *Dialectic of Modernity*, 2000), for whom the Holocaust could not have happened without modern industrial society and its bureaucracy. In this kind of society, authoritative legal guidelines and the breaking down of events into individual, rationally optimized processes both technically and morally enabled things which, if seen as an overall picture, would have scared away the parties involved. For this reason, to Bauman, the Holocaust was not the result of uncontrolled feelings but of the rationality of the modern state.

Schwartz provides many proofs and examples of this view, which extends far beyond genocide. Ethnic "cleansings" are for that reason a part of modernity and, with that said, also a part of the history of democracy. They cannot be simply assigned to dictators. As Carsten Kretschmann of the University of Stuttgart says, Schwartz correctly emphasizes that the comprehensive population exchange between Greece and Turkey, as was regulated in the 1923 Treaty of Lausanne, was if nothing else a work of two democratic states, namely France and Great Britain. And Churchill as well as Roosevelt saw their optional courses of action largely in relation to the world of experience brought on by Lausanne. Ethnic "cleansings" thus actually not only comprise a dark side of modernity. Rather, they are also the dark side of democracy, as the American sociologist Michael Mann once formulated it. (Carsten Kretschmann, "Logik des Barbarischen", *Frankfurter Allgemeine* 27 January 2014, http://www.faz.net/michael-schwartz-ethnische-saeuberungen-in-der-moderne-logik-des-barbarischen-12770061.html)

Schwartz addresses colonial genocide around 1900 in Southwest Africa, the Indian massacres of 1947, and our present Near East conflicts, to mention just a couple of examples. These examples cause one to surmise that completeness with respect to this topic cannot be readily achieved, even if the term were specified more precisely and rigidly limited.

Schwartz takes up quite rigorously the examples he chooses to discuss, handling them in a thorough manner. And he does this with respect to every ethnic "cleansing" that is surrounded by its own research debate. For instance, Schwartz examines the question of the genocide of Armenians and whether the displacement of Germans from Eastern Europe in 1945 fits under this rubric (he thinks so) or was a 'humane' and legally enacted resettlement (according to what were once socialist states).

Kretschmann writes:

> As a rule, however, Schwartz cleverly sets individual accents. This applies on the one hand to the "early places of learning," above all in the Balkans, nationalization and ethnic "cleansing" have sinisterly gone hand in hand since the early 19th century. On the other hand, his thesis is also applicable to World War I, the consequence of which was not only that colonial powers "returned home." Rather, people groups became victims of arbitrary treatment and violence: Armenians ("genocidal deportation"), Greeks ("deportation and genocide") and Jews ("impeded deportation"). Above all, however, his term applies to the racist displacement and resettlement policies of the National Socialist regime, in particular with respect to the killing of Jews." (Kretschmann, ibid)

Schwartz treats "'cleansing' settlement democracies" in America and Australia in the 19th century (189–202), genocide and deportation in colonies in such places as southwest Africa and the Philippines around 1900 (202–219), and how this spilled over into colonies within Europe (220–235). What followed was "national liberation through displacement" with respect to Muslims in the 19th century:

Serbia, Greece and Bulgaria (238–261); alternating projects of intervention and coexistence in Bosnia, Herzegovina, Croatia and Macedonia (261–297); and the culmination of this process in the 1912–1913 Balkan wars (298–309), where the victims were primarily Muslims in 1912 and Christians in 1913.

All parties to World War I at least played with the thought of ethnic "cleansing," whether as an "ordered population exchange" (309–318) or as displacement. The climax in World War I was the genocide of Armenians (61–98) and of Ottoman Greeks (98–114). Schwartz states:

> The concept of ethnic "cleansing" in the intellectual discourse of World War I was not the sole possession of a single party involved in the war. Between 1914 and 1919, the fronts escalated on all sides. What fascinated intellectuals and academics was the thought of organizing a post-war future with "clean" separations between nations and, with that, having peace, even thereby hoping to safeguard humanity. (60)

World War I brought on population movements of a magnitude that had been inconceivable up to that time. For instance, Czarist Russia itself deported 700,000 ethnic Germans and up to one million Jews from its western provinces to the east. The worst example of such excesses was surely the murder of Armenians by Turks.

According to Schwartz, there were three models (319–424) during the period between the World Wars. The first was the 1919 Versailles model with protection of minorities, which could, however, hardly be asserted. The second was the 1929 Moscow model with federalism and autonomy. Finally, the Lausanne Agreement envisioned peaceful population exchanges to avoid violent separation of ethnic groups but in reality ended in ethnic "cleansings."

The 1923 Lausanne Agreement separated "Turks" and "Greeks" (396–424), for instance, whereby the forced resettlement of two million people from two empires led to the creation of two nation-states. Similarly, from 1918 to 1925, 1.38 million Germans living in Poland migrated to the scaled-down German Empire.

The Third Reich and the Holocaust are naturally featured (425–466), but so are the resettlement agreements of World War II generally (467–491). The transfer plans of the anti-Hitler coalition follow (492–519). Stalin's punitive actions initially followed cries regarding class struggle, but then increasingly became ethnic "cleansings" (519–532). Schwartz provides a very good presentation on the movement of refugees during World War II and their displacement after World War II, with a total of two million deaths (532–564), and on the 1946–1950 forced resettlement of Germans from central and eastern Europe (564–578). In all, 31 million people in Central and Eastern Europe became the victims of forced migration policies (579). In parallel, there were 30 million victims of decolonization, including four million deaths (579–580).

Schwartz also examines the population exchange and displacement on the Indian subcontinent (580–599) after the British colony disintegrated into two states. This event and the post-World War II German resettlement are the two largest ethnic cleansings since 1945. Schwartz estimates a total of 17.5 million victims. Finally, Schwartz presents the situation in Israel and Palestine since 1947 (600–621).

Resettlements and population exchanges have often been planned as civil and sensible means of resolving conflict, but almost without exception they have slowly or not so slowly degenerated into violence. For instance, at the end of the British colonial era in India, theoretically all Muslims were released to resettle in Pakistan and Hindus were likewise released to leave Pakistan. Nevertheless, when the streams of resettlers brushed up against each other as they passed, the atmosphere heated up and eventually exploded into an unbelievable amount of bloodshed. (See the similar comment by Ernst Piper, "Staatenbildung als Gewaltakt: Michael Schwartz, *Ethnische 'Säuberungen' in der Moderne*," DeutschlandRadio Kultur, 20 May 2013, http://www.deutschlandradiokultur. de/staatenbildung-als-gewaltakt.1270.de.html?dram:article_id=247110).

It is very unfortunate that the book ends at around 1950, apart from relatively brief treatments of Palestine and the Indian subcontinent. What about eponymous Serbia? How does the thesis of modernity as a precondition for ethnic "cleansings" relate to events in Sudan, Turkey's dealings with the Kurds, or the actions of Islamic State in Syria and Iraq? One can only hope that the author will write another volume to bring his thesis up to date.

Prof Dr Dr Thomas Schirrmacher, Director, International Institute for Religious Freedom, Professor of the Sociology of Religion, Associate Secretary General of the World Evangelical Alliance

Persecution in 1 Peter: Differentiating and Contextualizing Early Christian Suffering
Travis B. Williams

Supplements to Novum Testamentum 145, Leiden / Boston: Brill, 2012, xxvii + 481 pp., hardbound, ISBN 978-90-04-24201-2, € 203.00, US$ 263.00.

Like no other book of the New Testament, 1 Peter addresses the suffering and persecution endured by the early Christians. The letter also affirms the believers' new status as the people of God and provides strategies for coping with such suffering. To understand 1 Peter, it is crucial to understand the readers' situation.

This comprehensive monograph, revised from the author's PhD dissertation at the University of Exeter, provides that service. It reconstructs with clarity and in great detail what is known of the recipients of 1 Peter and their situation as a religious minority in ancient Asia Minor.

One central question is the essence and scope of the suffering that these predominantly Gentile Christians faced. According to Williams, they encountered a number of social conflicts as a result of their conversion. The dynamics involved in these conflicts can be understood with reference to social psychology; the nature of the suffering addressed by 1 Peter can be understood by situating the letter against the backdrop of conflict management in first-century Asia Minor.

The introductory material includes a survey of prior research, a discussion of the difficulties involved in historical reconstruction, and a description of social conflict from a social-psychological perspective. Part one of the book then provides a social profile of the recipients so as to differentiate the readers' troubling experiences and contextualize the conflict situation by locating the various causes and numerous forms of conflict in first-century AD Asia Minor (327). The discussion covers the geographic setting of 1 Peter and the impact of Roman rule in Anatolia, and it then situates the addressees of the letter in this context, considering their ethnic composition and socio-economic status in relation to the economic situation in Anatolia. The readers live in an urban setting; most of them were in a precarious socio-economic situation. This information has important implications for understanding the dangers and threats which the readers faced.

Part two, "Contextualising the Conflict in 1 Peter," describes conflict management in Roman Anatolia. Williams distinguishes several action strategies (including physical violence, economic oppression and spiritual affliction) and third-party strategies (charges in and activities of civic and provincial courts). This part of Williams' study also includes an instructive survey of the legal status of Christians in the Roman world (179–236). Williams examines the relationship between Christians and the Roman state (including persecutions during the first century and again in the third century under Decius) and addresses the difficult question of reconciling the Christians' legal status and their experience of persecution. To achieve this task, Williams considers the nature of the Anatolian judicial process and the relationship between Christians and society. Although the Christians had "an effectively criminalized legal standing," they were exposed to escalated persecution only on sporadic occasions (331).

Against this backdrop, part three (239–326) examines the nature of the conflict in 1 Peter. Williams first addresses the causes of conflict related to the Christians' new behaviour, such as their social withdrawal from voluntary associations, the imperial cult and worship of the gods, as well as their distinctive lifestyle of good works aimed at pleasing God rather than at gaining social approval. In addition, he looks at their precarious legal status, in that their religious practice was effectively illegal. He then explores the various forms that this conflict may have taken (299–326). Explicit and implicit forms of conflict include verbal assault, physical abuse and legal actions; other possible, conjectured forms of suffering are tensions with spouses (e.g. between Christian wives and unbelieving husbands), economic oppression, social ostracism from the community in general, and spiritual affliction through curses or magic employed against believers.

Throughout the book, Williams combines meticulous socio-historical inquiry with insights from social psychology. Although it does not answer all questions, Williams' social-psychological approach sheds fresh light on the nature of the suffering addressed in the letter and on religious persecution in antiquity in general. His insights also enable readers to appreciate the ingredients and complexities of religious conflict in other contexts and ages, through his careful examination of social relations, legal conditions and economic as well as spiritual aspects. A helpful companion volume is P. A. Holloway, *Coping with Prejudice: 1 Peter in Social-Psychological Perspective* (WUNT 244; Tübingen: Mohr Siebeck, 2009), which addresses in detail how the readers were encouraged to cope in a Christian manner with the suffering so ably analysed in Williams' study.

Prof Dr Christoph Stenschke, Department of Biblical and Ancient Studies, University of South Africa

The Martyrs of Malatya
James Wright

Wyoming, MI: Evangelical Press, 2015, 216 pp., ISBN 978-1783971138, US $15.98.

The book describes the backgrounds of the three Christians killed in Malatya, Turkey on 18 April 2007. Necati Aydin was raised as a Sunni Muslim whilst Uğur Yuksel was raised within the Alevi tradition, a religious group whose beliefs combine elements of Shi'a Islam and pre-Islamic Anatolian practices. Tilmann Geske was raised in Germany.

Necati's story contains a number of interesting elements. Religious exploration began early in his life after a friend introduced him to the thinking of Fethullah Gulen. Necati was inspired, catching a dream of Islamic revival and a "future free of oppression, exploitation, violence, and all kinds of immorality" (p. 33). Later he met Shemse (a woman from a Christian background), who encouraged him to read the Injil, i.e. the New Testament. Necati made the decision to follow Jesus, and he later married Shemse. His passion for religious revival would find expression in his actively promoting Christ and urging others to read the Injil for themselves.

The book also describes the context of the Christian community within Turkey. It succinctly summarizes the historical origins of the deep sense of suspicion towards Turkish Christians that is prevalent to this day. One of the book's strong points is its demonstration of the deeply rooted factors within Turkish society that underlie the perpetrating of acts of violence against specific individuals. The book calls for tackling these underlying issues in order to address the religious freedom deficit experienced by many Turkish citizens. For this reason, I regard it as a valuable resource for those working on religious freedom matters. It calls on Turkey to acknowledge the historical origins of religious intolerance and to revise the religious education curriculum in state schools and the portrayal of religious diversity in popular media.

One weakness of the book is that some terms are used without being defined, notably 'Alevi.' This is a significant omission since the term is crucial to Uğur's story, although it is understandable since the book was first written in Turkish and the term would be widely understood in Turkey.

Two previous books covered the massacre of Malatya. Wolfgang Haede's *Faithful until Death: The Story of Necati Aydin, a Turkish Martyr for Christ* (2012) is a very factual report by a German pastor in Turkey about his Turkish brother-in-law. Jonathan Carswell's *Married to a Martyr: The Story of a Murdered Missionary in Turkey* (2008) describes the life of Susanne Geske, widow of Tilman Geske. Wright's book, meanwhile, attempts to put the story of the three murdered Christians in a broader context of Turkish history and society.

Jonathan Andrews, a researcher and writer on Middle East issues, Cheltenham, UK

The Silence of Our Friends:
The Extinction of Christianity in the Middle East
Ed West

Kindle Edition, 2013, ASIN: B00HDOF1DW 37 pp., US$ 2.99.

Ed West is deputy editor of the Catholic Herald, and this work has all the marks of a journalist. In a highly concentrated and rapid-fire way, the reader is taken on a tour of the Middle East and its threatened ancient communities, especially the Christians belonging to different confessional families.

West shows us how the present situation has resulted from the rise of radical Islamism and underscores the West's complicity in this development, at least in some places. He notes the West's frequent silence about the atrocities being committed in the name of Islam, which could be due to ignorance of the demographic situation, because Islamism is useful as a policy tool in the region or due to fear of retaliation.

The author describes well the complex pattern of Christian communities in the area and then, one by one, the horrors that have befallen them. Just as we are grasping the terrible condition of Iraqi Christians, we are given a litany of the woes of those in Syria and in Egypt. Although there is a good section on Turkey, representing the non-Arab world, there is no coverage of Iran and only passing references to Afghanistan and Pakistan.

Christians have long been bridge-builders in the Middle East and, for this reason alone, the West should take an interest in the survival of these communities. Moderate Muslims, too, if they wish for open and tolerant societies, should make sure that Christians survive. There have been some encouraging signs that this at last may be happening in countries like Egypt.

The Israeli exception is noted and Israel is commended for its relatively good policy on religious liberty, but West also observes that most Palestinian Christians blame Israeli policies for their plight rather than Islamist hostility towards them. Again, this may be because of fear of reprisals.

We have to ask: what are the seeds of these outbreaks of severe persecution? How are they rooted in the sources of Islam, in Islamic law and in contemporary writing on these subjects? By comparison with his forthright language in other areas, West is somewhat restrained in his description of the dhimma, the discriminatory legislation imposed on non-Muslims, and on repeated outbreaks of persecution throughout history. These form an important background to the recent atrocities and should therefore be mentioned.

The responses that he outlines in the final part of the book include vigorous advocacy by churches, NGOs and individuals in the West, pressure on Western governments to link bi-lateral relations with human rights issues, welcome for those fleeing persecution and providing 'safe havens' in at least some contexts. Each of these is controversial, but we are not going to help our brothers and sisters in the Middle East by being bland. That, certainly, Ed West is not.

A more detailed critical apparatus would have been useful in tracing some of the works to which reference is made. It is, however, very good to have a compact contribution of this kind which can easily be read electronically.

Bishop Michael Nazir-Ali, Oxford Centre for Training, Research, Advocacy and Dialogue (OXTRAD), London

I I R F   R e p o r t s

**A monthly journal with special reports,
research projects, reprints and documentation
published by the
International Institute for Religious Freedom
(Bonn – Cape Town – Colombo)**

www.iirf.eu/iirfreports

Guidelines for authors
Version 2020-1 (February 2020)

This document combines essential elements of the editorial policy and the house style of IJRF which can be viewed on www.iirf.eu.

Aims of the journal

The IJRF aims to provide a platform for scholarly discourse on religious freedom and religious persecution. The term persecution is understood broadly and inclusively by the editors. The IJRF is an interdisciplinary, international, peer reviewed journal, serving the dissemination of new research on religious freedom and contains research articles, documentation, book reviews, academic news and other relevant items.

Editorial policy

The editors welcome the submission of any contribution to the journal. All manuscripts submitted for publication are assessed by a panel of referees and the decision to publish is dependent on their reports. The IJRF subscribes to the Code of Best Practice in Scholarly Journal Publishing, Editing and Peer Review of 2018 (https://sites.google.com/view/assaf-nsef-best-practice) as well as the National Code of Best Practice in Editorial Discretion and Peer Review for South African Scholarly Journals (http://tinyurl.com/NCBP-2008) and the supplementary Guidelines for Best Practice of the Forum of Editors of Academic Law Journals in South Africa. As IJRF is listed on the South Africa Department of Higher Education and Training (DoHET) "Approved list of South African journals", authors linked to South African universities can claim subsidies and are therefore charged page fees.

Submission adresses

➤ Book reviews or suggestion of books for review: bookreviews@iirf.eu
➤ Noteworthy items and academic news: noteworthy@iirf.eu
➤ All other contributions: research or review articles, opinion pieces, documentation, event reports, letters, reader's response, etc.: editor@iirf.eu
   IJRF, POBox 1336, Sun Valley 7985, Rep South Africa

Selection criteria

All research articles are expected to conform to the following requirements, which authors should use as a checklist before submission:
➤ **Focus:** Does the article have a clear focus on religious freedom / religious persecution / suffering because of religious persecution? These terms are understood broadly and inclusively by the editors of IJRF, but these terms clearly do not include everything.

> **Scholarly standard:** Is the scholarly standard of a research article acceptable? Does it contribute something substantially new to the debate?
> **Clarity of argument:** Is it well structured, including subheadings where appropriate?
> **Language usage:** Does it have the international reader, specialists and non-specialists in mind and avoid bias and parochialism?
> **Substantiation/Literature consulted:** Does the author consult sufficient and most current literature? Are claims thoroughly substantiated throughout and reference to sources and documentation made?

Submission procedure

1. Submissions must be complete (see no.6), conform to the formal criteria (see no. 8-10) and must be accompanied by a cover letter (see no.3-4).
2. The standard deadlines for the submission of academic articles are 1 February and 1 August respectively for the next issue and a month later for smaller items such as book reviews, noteworthy items, event reports, etc.
3. A statement whether an item is being submitted elsewhere or has been previously published must accompany the article.
4. Research articles will be sent to up to three independent referees. Authors are encouraged to submit the contact details of 4 potential referees with whom they have not recently co-published. The choice of referees is at the discretion of the editors. The peer-review process is a double blind process. This means that you should not consult with or inform your referees at any point in the process. Your paper will be anonymized so that the referee does not know that you are the author. Upon receiving the reports from the referees, authors will be notified of the decision of the editorial committee, which may include a statement indicating changes or improvements that are required before publication. You will not be informed which referees were consulted and any feedback from them will be anonymized.
5. Should the article be accepted for publication, the author will be expected to submit a finalized electronic version of the article.
6. Include the following:
> An abstract of no more than 100 words.
> Between 3 and 10 keywords that express the key concepts used in the article.
> Brief biographical details of the author in the first footnote, linked to the name of the author, indicating, among others, year of birth, the institutional affiliation, special connection to the topic, choice of UK or American spelling, date of submission, full contact details including phone number and e-mail address.
7. Authors are expected to also engage with prior relevant articles in IJRF, the Religious Freedom Series, and IIRF Reports (www.iirf.eu) to an appropriate degree. So check for relevant articles as the peer reviewers will be aware of these.

8.   Articles should be spell-checked before submission, by using the spellchecker on the computer. Authors may choose either 'UK English' or 'American English' but must be consistent. Indicate your choice in the first footnote.

9.   Number your headings (including introduction) and give them a hierarchical structure. Delete all double spaces and blank lines. Use as little formatting as possible and definitely no "hard formatting" such as extra spaces, tabs. All entries in the references and all footnotes end with a full stop. No blank spaces before a line break.

10.   Research articles should have an ideal length of 4 000 words and a maximum of 6 000 words. Articles longer than that are not normally accepted, but may be published if, in the views of the referees, it makes an exceptionally important contribution to religious freedom.

11.   Research articles are honoured with two complimentary printed copies.

12.   For research articles by members of the editorial team or their relatives, the full editorial discretion is delegated to a non-partisan editor and they are submitted to the same peer review process as all other articles.

Style requirements

1.   IJRF accepts any consistently used citation style that is clearly defined named by the author. The historical citation style of the journal is the 'name-date' method (or Harvard system) for citations in the text.

2.   In the Harvard Style, a publication is cited or referred to in the text by inserting the author's last name, year and page number(s) in parentheses, for example (Mbiti 1986:67- 83). More detailed examples can be found on: www.iirf.eu > journal > instructions for contributors.

3.   Graphics (e.g. graphs, tables, photographs) will only be included in an article if they are essential to understanding the text. Graphics should not be included in the body of the article. Number graphics consecutively, save each in a separate file and indicate clearly in the text where each should be placed.

4.   Footnotes should be reserved for content notes only, unless a footnote based citation style is used. Bibliographical information is cited in the text according to the Harvard method (see 2 above). Full citations should appear in the References at the end of the article (see below).

5.   References should be listed in alphabetical order of authors under the heading "References" at the end of the text. Do not include a complete bibliography of all works consulted, only a list of references actually used in the text.

6.   Always give full first names of authors in the list of references, as this simplifies the retrieval of entries in databases. Keep publisher names short.

Subscriptions (for print version only!) 2016

Please note that the IJRF is *freely available on the web* a few weeks after publication at: www.iirf.eu and you can register for an email alert.

Annual subscription fee 2016 (2 issues):   **South African Rand 300**

Date: _____   VAT and postage included.

Name	
Address	
Postal/Zip Code	
Country	
Telephone	
Mobile	
Fax	
Email	

I/we wish to order *International Journal for Religious Freedom* starting with the year: 2013.

Please tick the appropriate   ☐ This is a new subscription   ☐ This is a renewal

☐ I/ we order the following **back issues** at Rand 150 per copy:

(NB: There was only one pilot issue in 2008)

☐ 1-1 (2008)   ☐ 2-1 (2009)   ☐ 2-2 (2009)   ☐ 3-1 (2010)   ☐ 4-1 (2011)   ☐ 4-2 (2011)
☐ 5-1 (2012)   ☐ 5-2 (2012)   ☐ 6-1/2 (2013)   ☐ 7-1/2 (2014)   ☐ 8-1/2 (2015)

☐ I have made an **electronic transfer** to the following account
(International: charge "all fees to sender" and add 5% for South African bank fees.)

☐ **Main Account South Africa:** Payment must be in Rand

International Institute for Religious Freedom Cape Town   **Account Number** 071 117 431
Bank Standard Bank   **Type of Account** Current Account
Branch Sea Point   **SWIFT Code** SBZAZAJJ
Branch Code 02 41 09   **Beneficiary reference** IJRF, Year, Name

☐ **For European Customers** (in Euro)   **Bank:** Volksbank Worpswede e.G., Germany
International Institute for Religious Freedom (SA)   **IBAN:** DE71291665680009701200
Account Number: 9701200   **BIC:** GENODEF1WOP
Bank Code/BLZ: 29166568   **Beneficiary reference** IJRF, Year, Name

---

☐ I have paid via **GivenGain**: http://iirfct.givengain.org **(preferred for international subscriptions); payment must be in RAND).**

☐ I enclose a cheque/postal order to the value of _____ ZAR made payable to International Institute for Religious Freedom Cape Town **(For foreign cheques add R 200 for bank charges).**

Return this form with your (proof of) payment to: subscriptions@iirf.eu

IJRF, P.O. Box 1336, Sun Valley, 7985, Rep South Africa, Tel +27-21 783 0823

Order Form for AcadSA Publications
Religious Freedom Series

Title	Unit Price*	Copies	Amount
Re-examining Religious Persecution: Constructing a Theological Framework for Understanding Persecution. Charles L Tieszen Religious Freedom Series, Vol 1	R 90		
Suffering, Persecution and Martyrdom: Theological Reflections. Christof Sauer and Richard Howell (editors) Religious Freedom Series, Vol 2	R 250		
		Total	

*Prices exclude shipping and handling.
  Bulk discounts on request

Personal Details

Name   Surname

Postal Address   Postal Code

Country

Telephone   E-Mail

Email, Fax or post this form to
AcadSA, P.O. Box 15918, Panorama, Parow 7506, Rep. South Africa
Tel: +27 21 839 1139, Fax: on request, Email: info@acadsa.co.za

www.acadsa.co.za

European Orders
Book publications of IIRF from the Religious Freedom Series and the Global Issues Series are also available in Germany from: any bookseller and most also on Amazon.